D1796316

CLAIT Plus 2006

Unit 1
Integrated e-Document Production

Using
Microsoft® Windows & Word XP

Release CP621v1

Published by:

CiA Training Ltd
Business & Innovation Centre
Sunderland Enterprise Park
Sunderland SR5 2TH
United Kingdom

Tel: +44 (0)191 549 5002
Fax: +44 (0)191 549 9005

info@ciatraining.co.uk
www.ciatraining.co.uk

ISBN 1 86005 311 4

First published 2005

CiA Training's guides for CLAIT Plus 2006 are a collection of structured exercises to provide support for each unit in the new qualification. The exercises build into a complete open learning package covering the entire syllabus, to teach how to use particular software applications. They are designed to take the user through the features to enhance, fulfil and instil confidence in the product.

UNIT 1: INTEGRATED E-DOCUMENT PRODUCTION - The guide supporting this core unit contains exercises covering the following topics.

- Understanding Files and Folders
- Importing Files
- Protecting Files
- Working with Tables
- Opening Closing and Saving Files
- Applying a House Style
- Printing Screen Layout
- Page Setup and Layout
- Mail Merge
- Headers and Footers
- Entering and Editing Data
- Bullets and Numbering
- Checking and Proof Reading
- Symbols
- Working with Fields
- Search and Replace
- Creating Documents

*Visit **www.ciasupport.co.uk** for hints, tips and supplementary information on published CiA products.*

This guide is suitable for:

- Any individual wishing to sit the OCR examination for this unit. The user works through the guide from start to finish. Some prior knowledge of *Windows* and *Word XP* would be useful, gained for example from working through the corresponding units produced by CiA for New CLAIT.

- Tutor led groups as reinforcement material. It can be used as and when necessary.

Aims and Objectives

To provide the knowledge and techniques necessary for the attainment of a certificate in this core unit. After completing the guide the user will be able to:

- Enter and Amend Data
- Perform Mail Merge
- Check Work for Accuracy
- Import and Manipulate Objects
- Apply Specified House Style to Files
- Work with Tables

Introduction

This guide was created using version *XP* of *Windows* and *Word*. It assumes that the programs have been correctly and **fully** installed on your personal computer. Some features described in this guide may not work if the program was not **fully** installed. *Windows XP* has a hierarchical system of users. Each user is given a particular status that governs what they can and cannot do. The types of user are: **Administrators**, **Power Users**, **Restricted Users**.

Important Notes For All Users

The CD accompanying this guide contains files to enable the user to practise new techniques without the need for data entry. These files must be copied to a designated folder on the hard drive so that all newly created files can be saved to the same location.

Note: *The CD automatically installs the data files by default into **My Documents** in a folder **CIA DATA FILES\Clait Plus 2006\Unit X** ...*

Notation Used Throughout This Guide

- Key presses are included within < > e.g. **<Enter>** means press the Enter key.

- Menu selections are written, e.g. **File | Open** means select the File option and then Open from the new menu.

- The guide is split into individual exercises. Each exercise consists of a written explanation of the feature, followed by a stepped exercise. Read the **Guidelines** and then follow the **Actions**, with reference to the **Guidelines** if necessary.

Recommendations

- Work through the exercises in sequence so that one feature is understood before moving on to the next.

- Read the whole of each exercise before starting to work through it. This ensures the understanding of the topic and prevents unnecessary mistakes.

Section 1

Manage Files and Folders

By the end of this Section you should be able to:

Understand Directory Structure

Recognise File Types

Delete Files

Use the Recycle Bin

Archive Files

Open, Close and Save Files

Create Screen Dumps

Print a Variety of Documents

Exercise 1 - Folders and Disks

Guidelines:

In order to assist in storing and finding files and programs on the hard disk, *Windows* uses **Folders**. The hard (or floppy) disk, or CD, is split into many folders, each containing all the files related to a specific task or program. A folder may also contain other folders, thus sub-dividing the disk even further. The concept is much like organising a filing cabinet by having separate drawers and files for each particular task.

A folder in *Windows* appears as an icon,   , with the name of the folder printed next to or underneath it, depending on the view displayed. When the icon is double clicked, the folder opens, and its contents are displayed.

Actions:

1. If the data files for this guide are stored within **My Documents** (see *Note* on page 4) then double click on the **My Documents** icon on the **Desktop** and keep navigating by double clicking until the **Unit 1 Windows XP Data** folder is displayed in the **View Pane** on the right. If the data files are stored in another location, double click either the icon for **My Computer** or **My Network Places** and navigate to the files.

2. Double click on the **Unit 1 Windows XP Data** folder to open it.

Note: The appearance of the **Toolbar** buttons can be varied using the **Text options** setting which is accessed from **View | Toolbars | Customize**. The diagrams in this guide were obtained with a **Text options** setting of **Selective text on right**.

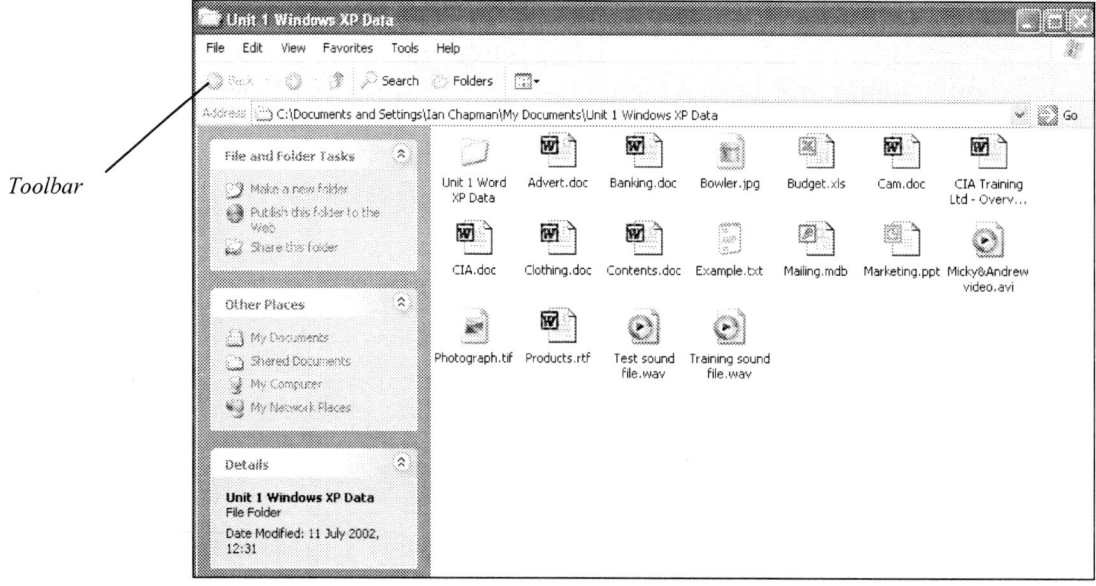

Toolbar

*The selected **View** is showing **Icons***

continued over

Exercise 1 - Continued

3. Select **View | Details** to see the files listed with more information.

Name ▲	Size	Type	Date Modified
Unit 1 Word XP Data		File Folder	10/03/2005 08:53
ADVERT.DOC	20 KB	Microsoft Word Doc...	09/07/2002 14:51
BANKING.DOC	20 KB	Microsoft Word Doc...	09/07/2002 14:51
Bowler.jpg	71 KB	JPEG Image	05/10/1999 08:34
Budget.xls	17 KB	Microsoft Excel Wor...	11/07/2002 12:06
CAM.DOC	20 KB	Microsoft Word Doc...	09/07/2002 14:52
CIA Training Ltd - Overview.doc	20 KB	Microsoft Word Doc...	28/07/1998 11:38
CIA.doc	22 KB	Microsoft Word Doc...	09/07/2002 14:53
CLOTHING.DOC	20 KB	Microsoft Word Doc...	09/07/2002 14:53
CONTENTS.DOC	20 KB	Microsoft Word Doc...	09/07/2002 14:53
Example.txt	1 KB	Text Document	05/12/1995 18:20
Mailing.mdb	112 KB	Microsoft Access Ap...	29/11/1999 14:36
Marketing.ppt	58 KB	Microsoft PowerPoi...	28/10/1999 12:41
Micky&Andrew video.avi	115 KB	Video Clip	12/12/1999 03:11
Photograph.tif	48 KB	Microsoft Office Do...	17/02/1993 11:24
Products.rtf	1 KB	Rich Text Format	13/06/2002 09:35
Test sound file.wav	19 KB	Wave Sound	31/01/1999 12:02
Training sound file.wav	16 KB	Wave Sound	31/01/1999 12:02

4. If the file extensions are not displayed, select **Tools | Folder Options** and click on the **View** tab. Make sure that the **Hide extensions for known file types** is <u>unchecked</u>. Click **OK** to display the file extensions.

5. There is one folder and 17 files displayed. The files represent 10 different types of files, the column may have to be clicked and dragged to see the file types:

.avi	is a video file
.wav	are sound files
.tif and **.jpg**	are image files
.doc	are *Word* documents
.txt	is a basic text file
.rtf (rich text format)	is a text file in a format that can be recognised by all computers regardless of the software installed
.xls	is an *Excel* workbook
.mdb	is an *Access* database
.ppt	is a *PowerPoint* presentation

Note: An object with a .exe extension, such as [image] *Psp.exe, is not a normal document/file, but an executable application, i.e. a program.*

6. Close any open folders using the **Close** button, [image], in each window.

Exercise 2 - Folder View

Guidelines:

Folder View governs the organisation of files and folders in any open window. It allows the easy viewing of the contents of disks/folders. It also helps control the copying, moving, creating and deleting of files and folders, known as **File Management**. In previous versions of *Windows* this function was carried out using *Windows Explorer*. This is still available and can be found under **Accessories**.

Actions:

1.   From the **Desktop** open the **My Computer** window.

2.   Click on the **Folders** button, Folders, on the toolbar to display the **Folders** pane. Click on **Local Disk (C:)** in the **Folders** pane to display its contents in the **View** pane on the right (only a single click is necessary from the **Folders** pane).

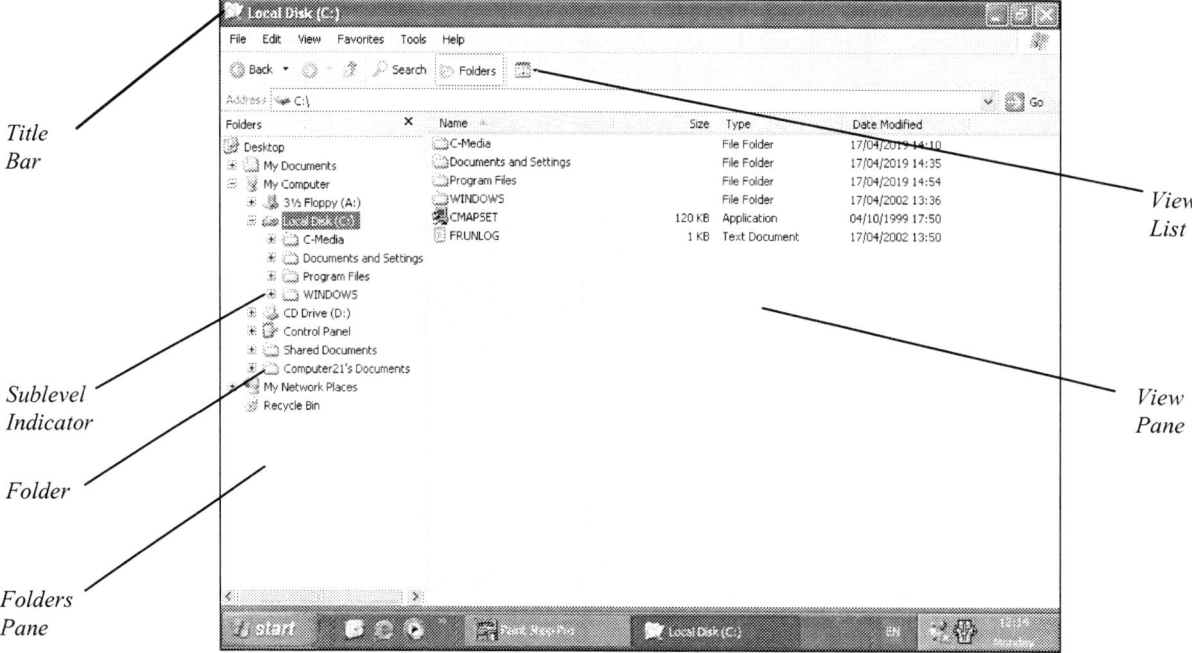

Title Bar

Sublevel Indicator

Folder

Folders Pane

View List

View Pane

Note: *The contents will be different to that above. There are also different views of the same information. The window above is viewed showing **Details**.*

3.   On the left is the **Folders** pane, which shows the drives and folders on the computer. On the right is the **View** pane, showing the contents of the selected drive or folder. Scroll through the list of drives and folders in the **Folders** pane.

continued over

Exercise 2 - Continued

4.   Click on any folder icon in the **Folders** pane. The contents of the folder are shown in the **View** pane.

5.   Select **View | Thumbnails**. The folder contents are now shown as small pictures.

6.   Select **View | Details**. The folder contents now have their name, size, type and date modified displayed. This enables the smallest, largest, newest, oldest and files of the same type to be identified.

7.   In the **Folders** pane, scroll to **My Documents** (or wherever the supplied data is saved), it has a ⊞ icon denoting that the folder has subfolders. Click once on the ⊞. The subfolders are displayed underneath the folder and the icon changes to a ⊟. This is called *expanding* a folder.

8.   Expand the **CIA DATA FILES** folder, and then the folders within it until you can see the **Unit 1 Windows XP Data** folder. Expand this folder; it contains one sub folder.

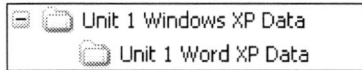

9.   To hide the subfolders, click on the ⊟ icon next to **Unit 1 Windows XP Data**. The icon changes to ⊞ again and the subfolders are hidden. This is called *collapsing* a folder.

10.   Click on the **Unit 1 Windows XP Data** folder to display the files in it. Make sure the view is **Details**.

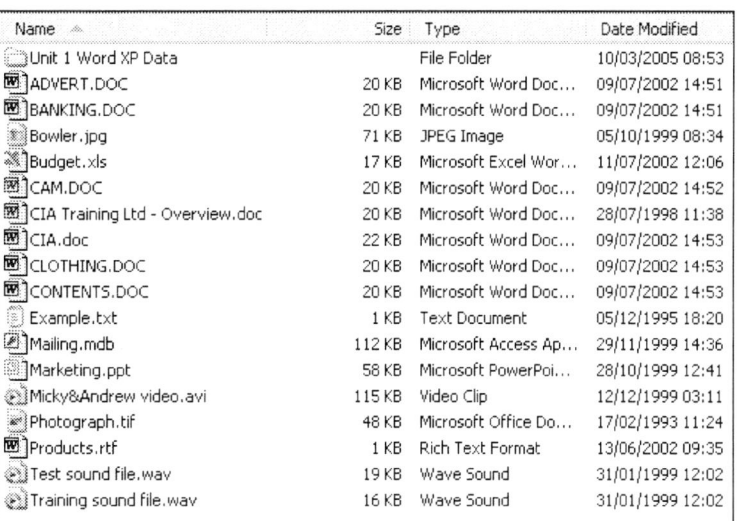

11.   Different types of files are displayed with a different icon before the name and the size, type and date when saved (modified) are all displayed.

12.   Identify each of the file types in this folder just by the icon and filename extension. Leave the window open for the next exercise.

Exercise 3 - Deleting Files

Guidelines:

Files and folders can be deleted in four main ways:

- Select the icon by clicking it, then press the <**Delete**> key.

- Click once on the file / folder with the **right** mouse button then select **Delete**.

- Click and drag the file / folder over the **Recycle Bin** icon on the desktop or in **Folders** view, , then release the icon "into" the bin (the Recycle Bin is covered in the next exercise).

- Select the file and click on the **Delete** button on the toolbar.

Note: *The result of deleting files depends on where the files are located. If the file is on a hard disk, then the file is removed (after a confirmation prompt), and placed in the Recycle Bin. If the file is on a floppy disk, a message appears checking if the user is sure that the file is to be deleted, as it will be deleted permanently.*

Actions:

1. In the **View** pane, click on the **Clothing** icon to select it, if not already selected. Press the <**Delete**> key. A message appears, confirming that the file is to be removed.

Confirm File Delete

Are you sure you want to send 'CLOTHING.DOC' to the Recycle Bin?

Yes   No

2. Clicking **Yes** would move the file to the **Recycle Bin**, but for now select **No**.

3. Click once on the **Clothing** icon with the **right** mouse button, then select **Delete** from the shortcut menu. At the message, select **No** to keep the file.

4. Click and drag the **Clothing** icon over the **Recycle Bin** icon in the **Folders** window and release the mouse button.

5. The icon disappears from the **View** pane and the file is moved to the **Recycle Bin**. Delete the **Cam** and **Mickey&Andrew video** files from **Unit 1 Windows XP Data**, using any of the above methods.

Note: *If a folder is deleted, a **Confirm Folder Delete** message is displayed, click **Yes** to move the folder and all its contents to the **Recycle Bin**.*

Exercise 4 - The Recycle Bin

Guidelines:

When files or folders are deleted, they are not instantly removed from the hard disk. They are held in the **Recycle Bin**, whose icon can be seen on the desktop or in any **Folders** pane. The Recycle Bin desktop icon changes according to whether it contains any files, [Recycle Bin], or is empty, [Recycle Bin]. All deleted items are stored there until the **Recycle Bin** is emptied. Until then, the files can be restored to their original location.

Once the **Recycle Bin** is emptied the contents are **permanently** deleted and **can no longer be recovered**. Deleting individual items from the **Recycle Bin** also permanently removes them.

Note: *Files or folders deleted from a floppy disk are **not** held in the **Recycle Bin**, but are deleted instantly.*

Actions:

1. Click the **Recycle Bin** icon in any **Folders** pane to display its contents, a list of all items that have been deleted.

Note: *The content of the **Recycle Bin** is dependant on when it was last emptied. The files **Clothing, Cam** and **Mickey&Andrew video** will be in the **Recycle Bin**, however, you may need to scroll to see them.*

2. Click the **Folders** button to close the **Folders pane** and the **Restore pane** is displayed in its place. There are options to **Restore** all the listed files and to **Empty** the entire **Recycle Bin** (permanently delete all the listed files and folders).

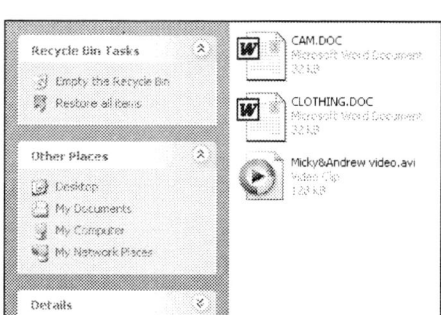

3. To restore a file or a folder, select it from the list, the **Restore all items** text will change to **Restore this item**. Click the **Clothing.doc** item and click **Restore this item**, the file is removed from the **Recycle Bin** and placed where it was before deletion (missing folders are recreated if necessary).

4. Close the **Recycle Bin** window.

5. Click with the **right** mouse button on the **Recycle Bin** icon on the **Desktop**. From the shortcut menu, select **Empty Recycle Bin**. A message appears confirming the action. Normally, you would select **Yes**, but in this case, to protect documents from deletion, select **No**.

Exercise 5 - Archiving Files

Guidelines:

One reason for archiving is to free up hard disk space. As space is limited on all computers, you must be aware that the disk space should be checked regularly and you must have a system for archiving old data.

However, there are also data security reasons. An organisation needs to consider the possibility of total file loss or corruption due to: a serious hardware fault, physical damage to the computer (possibly as a result of fire), infection by computer virus, accidental deletion and emptying of the **Recycle Bin**, theft or other malicious action.

The loss of vital files may be inconvenient to an individual using a home PC for hobby purposes, but to a business user, large or small, the loss could well be catastrophic. This makes it essential for regular, complete copies to be made of all files, which are identified as being critical to an organisation. This is known as **backing up** files and may be done at any time. Regular backing up ensures that even in the event of a total loss of data, an organisation has an almost current, duplicate set of its most important files, which it can rely upon to maintain business continuity.

Storage containing the backed up material is known as **backing store** and should be considered valuable. The fundamental reason for backing up files is to ensure that they cannot be lost, or completely destroyed, while saved on the hard drive of the PC or the file server. This means that it is not totally secure to keep the backing store in the same room, or even building, as the source material because of the risk of fire.

For absolute security, the backing store should be removed from the working environment (off site) and more than one set of backing store media should be used in rotation. All backup media should be kept in a storage environment which is theft-proof, fireproof and waterproof.

Archived data, which is <u>removed</u> from the computer on to CD or floppy disk, should also be treated as carefully as normal backing store.

Actions:

1.   Obtain a blank, formatted floppy disk and insert it into the floppy disk drive.

Note: *If you do not have access to a floppy disk (or disk drive), read this exercise for information.*

2.   Click on the ⊞ next to **My Computer** so 🖫 3½ Floppy (A:) can be seen.

continued over

Exercise 5 - Continued

3. Display the contents of the **Unit 1 Windows XP Data** folder in **Folder View**.

4. Right click on the subfolder **Unit 1 Word XP Data**. You are to make an archive copy of this folder and all of its contents.

5. Select **Copy** from the shortcut menu.

6. Now right click on the floppy disk icon in the **Folders** pane and select **Paste** from the menu. The folder and files are copied to the floppy disk.

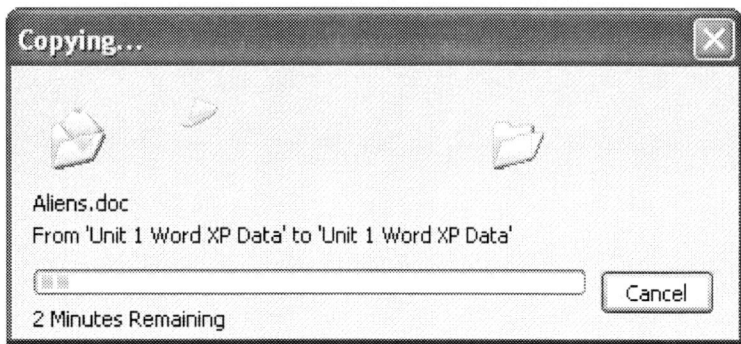

7. Click on the ⊞ at the left of the floppy disk icon. The **Unit 1 Word XP Data** folder has been backed up to the floppy disk.

8. Click on the folder in the **Folders** pane to reveal the files.

9. View the contents of **Unit 1Word XP Data** <u>within **My Documents**</u>.

10. Remove the floppy disk from the drive and leave **Folder view** open.

Exercise 6 - Opening and Closing Files

Guidelines:

Files can be opened directly from **Folder View**, provided the software in which they were created is installed on the computer.

Actions:

1. View the contents of the **Unit 1 Windows XP Data** folder in **Folder View**.

2. Double click the icon for the **Budget** file, 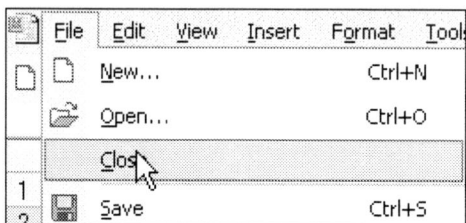. The application *Excel* starts, opening the **Budget** file.

3. To close the file, click the **File** menu and select **Close**.

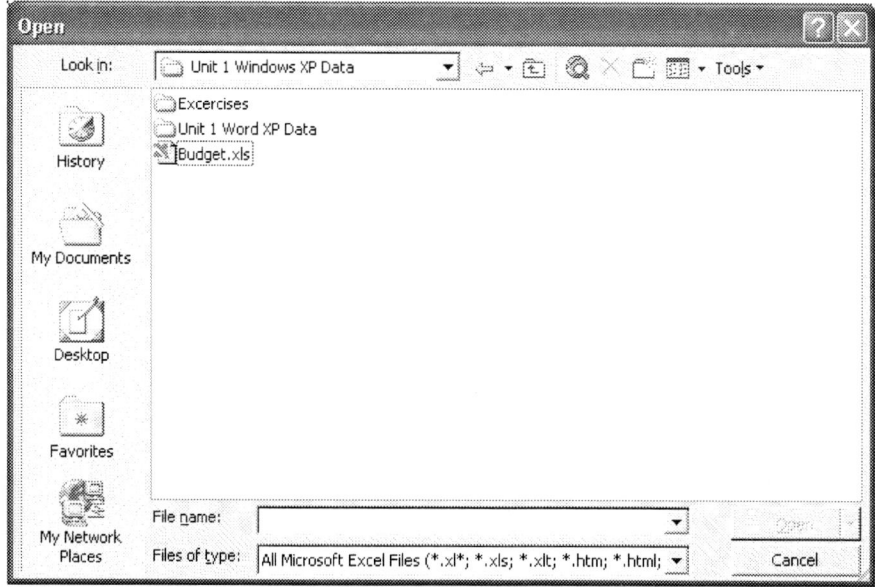

4. *Excel* is still open. To open the **Budget** file again, click the **Open** button, ⬚.

5. Make sure **Look in** the **Open** dialog box shows the **Unit 1 Windows XP Data** folder.

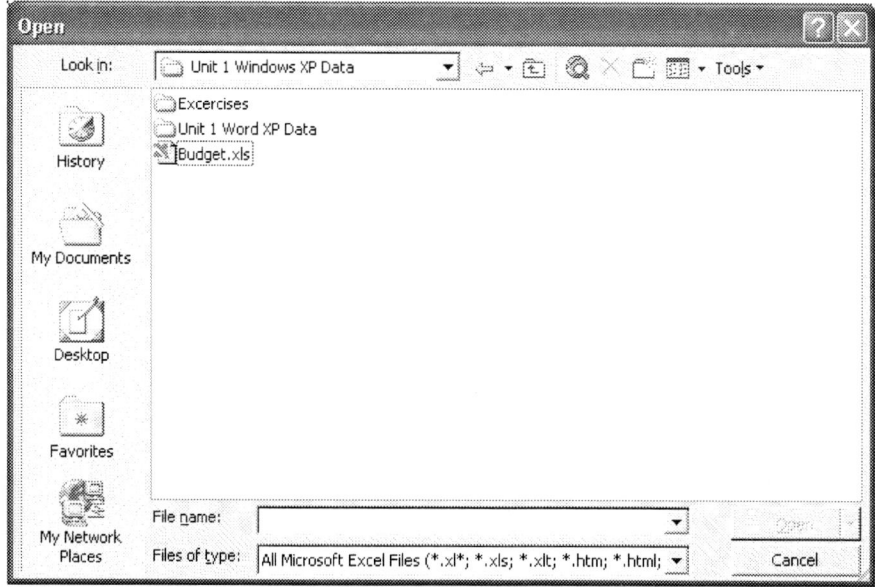

6. Select the file **Budget.xls** and click **Open**.

continued over

Exercise 6 - Continued

7. Close the file and *Excel* by clicking the **Close** button, , in the top right corner of the screen.

8. In **Folder View**, double click on the icon. *PowerPoint*, a presentation graphics application starts.

9. Use one of the methods learned to close *PowerPoint*.

10. Double click on to view this picture file. It is saved in **.jpg** format, one of the many picture formats available.

11. Close the application.

12. In turn, open the following files from **Folder View** and then close them: **Products**, a text file and **Mailing**, a database.

13. Leave **Folder View** open.

Exercise 7 - Saving Files

Guidelines:

A file must be saved if it is to be used again. However, if disk space is an issue, consider how important it is before saving a file. There are two main ways to save, depending on whether the file has been newly created, or whether it has previously been saved and given a name. You should be aware of where the data associated with this guide is located. The file you are about to save should be saved to the same location.

Actions:

1. From **Folder View**, open the file named **Products**. Position the cursor at the end of the text and type **For more information on the company, visit our website: www.ciatraining.co.uk**.

2. This file is to be saved with a different name, so that the original is not affected. Select the **File** menu and choose the **Save As** command. The **Save As** dialog box will then appear. The contents of the dialog box will vary between computers, but the diagram below shows an example of how it may look.

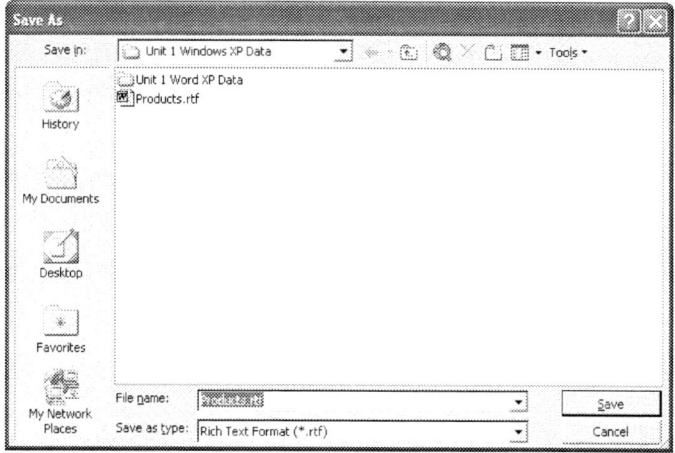

3. The file must be given a new name. Enter **Saving** in the **File name** box (the highlighted text will automatically be deleted).

4. Use the drop down list from the **Save in** box to locate the area where your documents are to be saved. Consult your tutor if you are not sure.

5. Click the **Save** button, [Save], at the bottom right of the dialog box. The chosen name now appears in the **Title Bar**.

*Note: A previously named document can be saved to the same location under the same name by clicking the **Save** button, [💾], on the Toolbar. The original version of the file will be overwritten. When a new file is to be saved, selecting **Save** also displays the **Save As** dialog box.*

6. Leave the application open.

Exercise 8 - Producing Evidence

Guidelines:

As part of the assessment for this unit, you will be required to make a printout of various settings applied. This is to demonstrate that you have set the options specified.

Actions:

1. With the **Saving** file open, select **File | Save As**. The **Save As** dialog box shows that this file has been saved in rich text format: **.rtf** (**Save as type**).

2. To make a copy of what you can see on the screen (this is called a screen dump), press the <**Print Screen**> key at the top right of the keyboard.

*Note: The key press <**Alt Print Screen**> captures the active dialog box rather than the full screen.*

3. Close the dialog box.

*Note: The image is copied to the Windows **Clipboard**.*

4. Start a new document by clicking ⬜. To paste in the image, click the **Paste** button, 📋. The page now shows the screen dump.

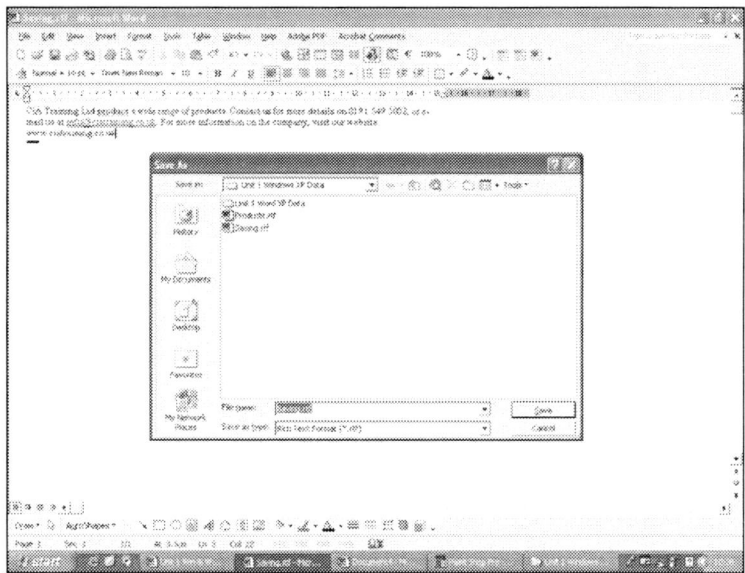

5. Beneath the image, type **Evidence of saving a file**.

Note: This image can be manipulated like other inserted images, e.g. click and drag a corner handle to resize it.

6. Save the document as **Evidence** and close it. Close any open documents.

Exercise 9 - Printing Documents

Guidelines:

Documents can be printed directly from **Folder view**, without opening the appropriate software application first.

Actions:

1. Use **Folder view** to display the contents of the **Unit 1 Word XP Data** folder, within the **Unit 1 Windows XP Data** folder.

2. Double click on the file **Invoice**. This is a typical business document for a company providing goods or services.

3. Select **File | Print Preview** to check how the document will look before printing, then close **Print Preview**.

4. Click the **Print** button, , to print a copy of the document.

5. Close the document and close *Word*.

6. Documents do not have to be opened before they can be printed. Right click on the file **Payroll**.

7. Select **Print** from the shortcut menu (the diagram below may show more options than exist on your menu).

Open
New
Print
Convert to Adobe PDF
Convert to Adobe PDF and EMail
Combine in Adobe Acrobat...
Open With ▶
WinZip ▶
Send To ▶
Cut
Copy
Create Shortcut
Delete
Rename
Properties

Note: *If you are prompted to save the file, select* **No**.

8. Use either method shown above to print the following documents: **Fax** and **Business Letter**.

Exercise 10 - Revision

1. Use **Folder View** to make a backup copy of the following files from the **Unit 1 Windows XP Data** folder: **Photograph.tif** and **Test sound file.wav**.

2. Create a screen dump of the file structure showing the contents of **Unit 1 Word XP Data** in **Details** view.

3. Save the evidence document as **Revision10**.

4. List the file types in the **Unit 1 Word XP Data** folder.

5. Display the contents of the **Unit 1 Windows XP Data** folder.

6. Delete the file **Bowler** from the **Unit 1 Windows XP Data** folder.

7. Close any open windows.

Note: Answers for this exercise are listed in the Answer section at the end of this guide.

Section 2

Enter and Amend Data

By the end of this Section you should be able to:

Insert and Delete Text and Numbers

Cut, Copy and Paste Text

Move Text

Check Spelling and Grammar

Add Headers and Footers to a Document

Protect Files

Use English Date Formats

Work with and Update Fields

Exercise 11 - Entering Text and Numbers

Guidelines:

One of the most widely used applications on computers is **Word Processing**. The following sections of this guide are concerned with one of the most popular word processing applications, *Microsoft Word*, starting with the process of data entry.

The keyboard is called an **input device** because it is used to input information to the computer. In a word processing application, any key pressed on the keyboard will appear in the document at the **Insertion Point**, where the cursor flashes. Each letter, number or symbol typed in is called a **character**.

The cursor can be moved by clicking the mouse pointer or by using the arrow keys on the keyboard. Text is entered at the cursor position, when the edge of the paper is reached, the text automatically wraps to the next line. Only press <**Enter**> if a new paragraph is to be started, or a new line is required before you reach the end of the current one. If a capital letter or a symbol at the top of a key, e.g. **%**, **£**, **@**, **?**, is required, hold down the <**Shift**> key while typing it.

Actions:

1. Start *Word XP* by selecting **Start | All Programs | Microsoft Word**.

2. Enter the following text. Type carefully and accurately to try and avoid any mistakes:

    Do you need help with I.T? CIA Training Ltd is a specialist computer training company, based in the north east of England. It has been trading for over sixteen years and has recently moved to new, larger premises in Sunderland.

    The company is involved in training in all computer software applications and is also a major producer of Open Learning materials for computer software. More details are available by telephoning (0191) 549 5002. Alternatively, you can e-mail us at info@ciatraining.co.uk.

3. To save the new document, select **File | Save As**.

4. Select the required location from the **Save in** box, the **Unit 1 Word XP Data** folder within **Unit 1 Windows XP Data**.

5. Enter the name **IT Specialists** in the **File name** box and click **Save**.

6. Close the document by selecting **File | Close**.

7. Leave *Word* open for the next exercise.

Exercise 12 - Inserting and Deleting Text

Guidelines:

Both the mouse and the cursor keys can be used to move the insertion point. Mistakes can be erased, or text inserted wherever required.

Actions:

1. Open the document **Theft**. This document can be found in the folder **Unit 1 Word XP Data**, which is a subfolder within the **Unit 1 Windows XP Data** folder. All documents and associated files for this part of the guide will be found here.

2. Click in the word **eleven** in the second sentence of the first paragraph.

3. Characters to the left of the cursor are deleted by pressing the **<Backspace>** key and characters to the right of the cursor are deleted using the **<Delete>** key. Delete the word **eleven** using these key presses.

4. In its place, type in **twelve**.

5. Make the following alterations to the document, by inserting and deleting text as necessary: First paragraph, first sentence: change **Hall** to **Manor**.

6. Second paragraph, first sentence: insert a space in **eachcase**.

7. Second paragraph, first sentence: change **wood stolen** to **wood has been stolen**.

8. Third paragraph, last sentence: change **continues** to **is continuing**.

9. Save the document as **Solved**.

10. Close the document.

Exercise 13 - Cut, Copy and Paste

Guidelines:

The **Cut, Copy** and **Paste** commands allow text to be moved around a document, from one place to another, quickly and easily. When text is cut, it is removed from its original location; when copied, the original is untouched.

When copied or cut, text is placed in a temporary storage area known as the **Clipboard**. Up to **24** cut or copied items can be held on the **Clipboard**.

Actions:

1.   Open the document **Organiser**.

2.   Make sure the **Task Pane** is visible: select **View | Task Pane**.

3.   From the **New Document** task pane, click on the drop-down arrow at the top of the pane, and select **Clipboard**.

4.   Because the **Clipboard** is shared between all *Office* applications, there may already be some items on it. If so, click the **Clear All** button, Clear All.

5.   Click and drag to highlight the first sentence **Mr Nelson rings...** and click the **Cut** button, ✄. An icon representing the cut text appears on the **Clipboard**.

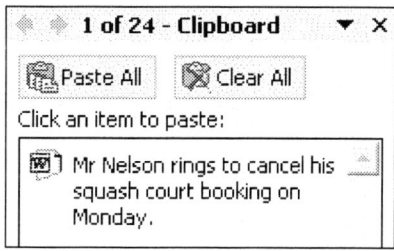

6.   Move the cursor to the end of the document and start a new line.

7.   Click the **Paste** button, 📋, to place the cut text at the insertion point.

8.   Select the sentence which is now at the top of the page: **John Weston wants....**

9.   Click the **Copy** button, 📋. The copied text is placed on the clipboard, next to the first item. Filling the clipboard in this way is known as **Collect and Paste**.

10. Paste this text at the end of the document, by clicking the first item in the **Clipboard**. Notice how the original text is untouched.

continued over

Exercise 13 - Continued

11. Continue to **cut** items from the top of the page until the **Clipboard** is full.

12. Position the cursor at the end of the document and select **Paste All**, [Paste All], to paste each cut item back into the document. The spacing may need to be adjusted.

13. Items can easily be deleted from the **Clipboard**. Click the **Clear All** button, [Clear All].

14. Close the **Clipboard** task pane.

15. Close the document <u>without</u> saving.

Exercise 14 - Moving and Copying Text

Guidelines:

The **Drag and Drop** facility speeds up the process of moving text from one location to another within a document. It is best used to move small amounts of text, cut and paste works better with larger areas.

Actions:

1.   Open the document **Grand Canyon**.

2.   Select the first sentence and move the mouse over the text until it becomes an arrow.

> Around six million years ago, the Colorado River in Arizona, U.S. began to carve a gorge through the landscape. That gorge became what we know today as the Grand Canyon. The Canyon is around 217 miles long, over a mile deep and 4 miles wide at;

3.   Click and hold down the mouse button, then drag the mouse to the end of the text. As the text is being dragged, the cursor becomes and the **Status Bar** reads **Move to where?**. A vertical line appears where the text will be inserted.

4.   Release the mouse to drop the text at the end of the document.

*Note: The drag and drop feature becomes drag and copy if the **<Ctrl>** key is held down whilst the text is being dragged. The cursor appears as and the **Status Bar** reads **Copy to Where?***

5.   Select the sentence that has just been moved.

6.   Hold down **<Ctrl>** and drag to the beginning of the text before releasing the mouse.

7.   The text is copied to the beginning of the document. You may have to insert a space. Check the end of the document for the same sentence.

8.   Obtain a printed a copy of the document.

9.   Practise moving and copying within this document using this technique.

10.   Close the document <u>without</u> saving.

Exercise 15 - Automatic Spell Checking

Guidelines:

Word has a large dictionary. Words not in the dictionary can be added but you will not need to do this. There are two main ways of spell checking. <u>Either</u> spell check while typing, <u>or</u> use the **Spelling Checker**.

Misspelled words are shown with a wavy red line underneath. Green wavy lines refer to grammatical errors.

Actions:

1. Open the document **Aliens**. For now, ignore grammatical errors.

2. If there are red and green wavy lines beneath some of the text, then the **Automatic Spelling & Grammar** feature is turned on. **Move to Step 5**. If not, follow the following steps.

3. Select **Tools | Options** and select the **Spelling and Grammar** tab.

4. Under **Spelling Check spelling as you type** should have a check mark against it, as should **Always suggest corrections** and **Check grammar as you type** under **Grammar**. If they don't, click in the appropriate white box to place the tick. Click **OK**.

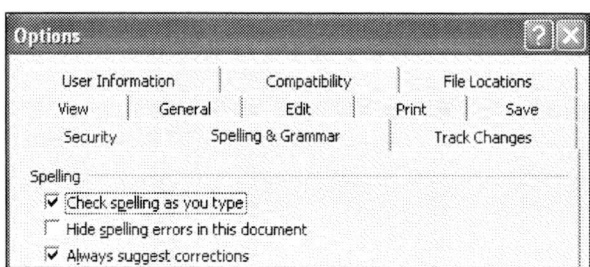

5. The quickest way of correcting errors is by using the mouse. Place the mouse over the first item underlined in red, **aproached** and click with the <u>right</u> mouse button. A shortcut menu appears. Suggestions are given in a list, in this case there is only one suggestion.

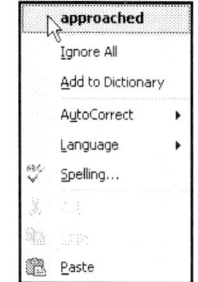

6. Select the correct spelling by clicking with the <u>left</u> mouse button. The error is corrected.

7. When text is being entered, a **Spell Book** is shown in the **Status Bar**. If there are mistakes, [image] appears, if everything is correct, [image].

8. Continue to correct the spelling errors in the same way. One is not a spelling error, but a repeated word, **saw saw**. Select **Delete Repeated Word**.

9. Print the document and close it <u>without</u> saving.

Exercise 16 - Spell Checker

Guidelines:

Another way to check spelling is to use the **Spelling and Grammar** dialog box.

Actions:

1. Open the document **Aliens** again. Make the title **Unexplained** bold.

2. Spelling errors are underlined in red and grammatical errors in green. With the cursor at the beginning of the first paragraph, click the **Spelling and Grammar** button, 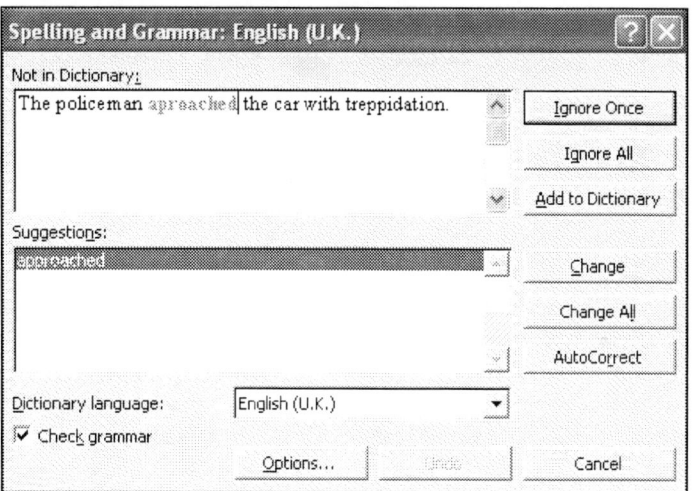, or select **Tools | Spelling and Grammar**. The **Spelling and Grammar** dialog box appears.

3. The first error is shown in the top area. Suggested alternatives are shown beneath. Errors can be ignored, changed or added to the dictionary. Select the alternative **approached** and click **Change**.

4. The next error appears. Work through the document, making corrections as necessary. Click **Ignore Once** for the green grammatical errors for the moment. For repeated words click **Delete**. The following message appears when the check is complete.

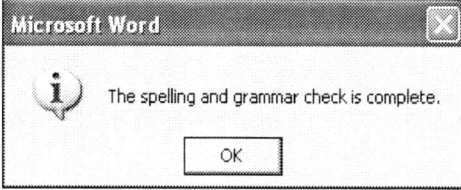

5. Click **OK** and save the document as **Correct** before closing it.

*Note: If the word required does not appear in the **Suggestions** box, it may be typed into the upper area of the Spelling and Grammar dialog box, correcting the error, and then **Change** selected.*

Exercise 17 - Grammar Checker

Guidelines:

Grammar is also checked as text is entered. *Word* makes suggestions which, like spelling suggestions, can be accepted or ignored.

Actions:

1. Open the document **Initiatives**.

2. The grammatical errors are underlined in green (it may take a few seconds for the errors to appear after the file is opened, if they don't appear quickly, double click at the end of the document). Click the **Spelling and Grammar** button, .

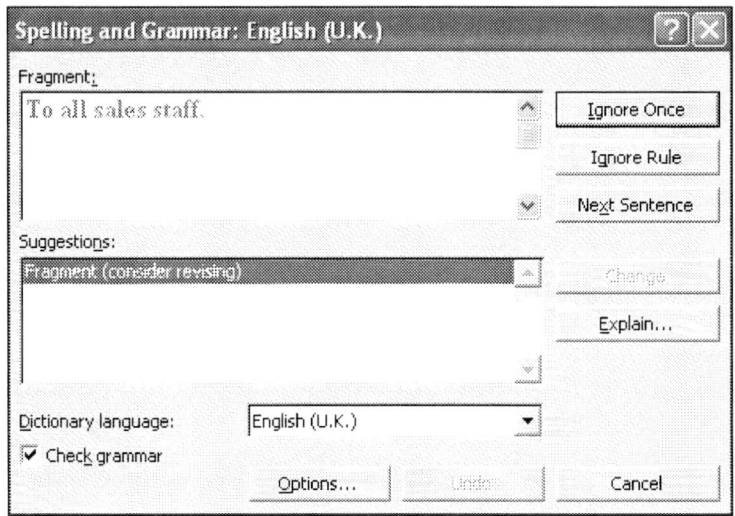

3. Notice how the buttons at the right of the dialog box are slightly different to when spelling is checked. Click **Next Sentence**.

4. The second error finds an extra space before the **?**. Click **Change** to accept the suggestion.

5. The third error is a little trickier in that a full stop has mistakenly been placed in the middle of a sentence. Click **Ignore Once** for now, but remember where it is. Move the dialog box, if necessary, to view the error.

6. Click **OK** when the grammar check is complete. Go back to the full stop error and delete it. Check that the **Spell Book** is showing all complete, .

7. Save the document as **Corrected** and close it.

Note: *It is good practice to proof read a document, even after it has been spell and grammar checked.*

Exercise 18 - Headers and Footers

Guidelines:

Headers and Footers are common identification lines at the top and bottom of each page. Such text at the top of a page is called a **Header** and at the bottom, a **Footer**. **Headers** and **Footers** can be added on alternate pages, or the same header/footer can be applied to every page. Special features such as the date, time and page numbering can be added to a **Header** or **Footer**.

Actions:

1.　Open the file **Hardware**.

2.　Check under **File | Page Setup | Layout** that neither **Different odd and even** nor **Different first page** is checked for **Headers and footers**. Click **OK**.

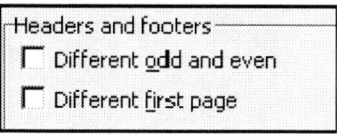

3.　Select **View | Header and Footer** to reveal the **Header and Footer** toolbar.

4.　Notice how the main document becomes ghosted. Create a centred two line **Header** by entering **<Tab> Computers Today <Enter> <Tab> By A Modem**.

5.　Select the **Switch Between Header and Footer** button, ⬚, to switch to the **Footer**.

6.　Add **CLAIT Plus News** as a centred **Footer** then click ⬚ to close the **Header and Footer** toolbar.

7.　**Print Preview** the document to check the appearance of the **Headers** and **Footers**.

Note: Headers and Footers are not visible in Normal document view - to see them, use either Print Preview or View | Print Layout.

8.　Print a copy of the document.

Note: Some printers do not print to the bottom of the page, so the Footer may not be visible in the Preview. To enlarge the Footer, select File | Page Setup |Layout and increase the setting for the Footer from the From edge area.

9.　Close the document <u>without</u> saving any changes.

Exercise 19 - Fields

Guidelines:

Fields are used for many different tasks, such as inserting codes, e.g. the date, into documents, automatic numbering of tables, figures and lists. Fields are also used in mail merging to produce personalised documents and to insert information. Fields can be added to a document header or footer to be printed with the document. When working with fields, either the field codes or the actual contents of the fields can be displayed.

Actions:

1. Click the **New Blank Document** button, ⬜, on the toolbar to start a new document.

2. Select **Tools | Options | View**. Ensure the **Show** area has the **Field codes** option checked. Select **Always** from the **Field shading** area and click **OK**.

3. Select **Insert | Date and Time**. Notice the available date formats. Some are commonly used in the United States. For the purposes of this assessment it is important to use English date formats, e.g. **dd/mm/yy**.

4. Choose the date in the correct format (**dd/mm/yy**). Make sure **Update automatically** is checked.

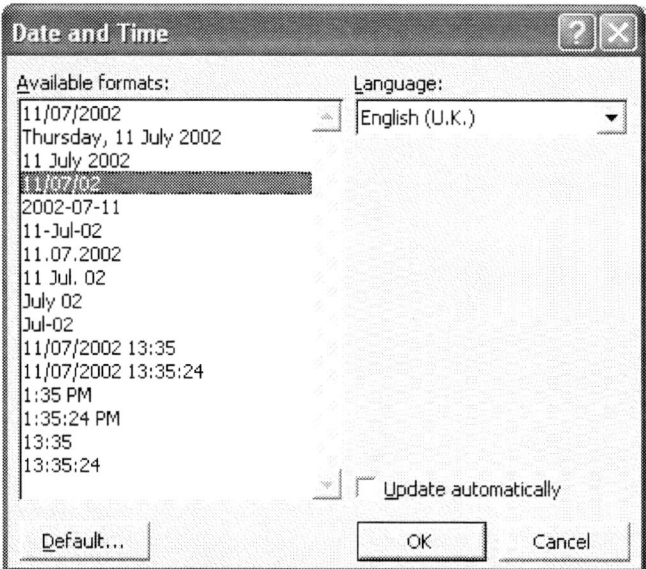

5. Click **OK**. Fields are recognised by **{ }** around the codes.

continued over

Exercise 19 - Continued

6. Notice how the **code** for the date can now be seen. When the document is printed or previewed this is converted into today's date.

7. Select **Tools | Options | View** and uncheck **Field codes**. Click **OK**. The date is now displayed, rather than the code.

8. Press **<Alt F9>**. This is a quicker way to toggle between displaying **Field codes** or their values. Press **<Alt F9>** again to display values.

9. General fields can also be used. Press **<Enter>** twice. Press **<Ctrl F9>**.

10. Between the brackets, type **Name** then click outside the field. This type of field is known as a **Comment** field and would be replaced by the required text.

11. Select **File | Properties** and change the **Author** to your own name, then click **OK**. Press **<Enter>** twice.

12. Select **Insert | Field** and from the **Categories** choose **Document Information**, then **Author** from **Field names**. Click **OK**. Press **<Alt F9>** to view the **Field codes**.

13. Experiment with other fields, then close the document <u>without</u> saving.

Note: *Field codes are deleted by highlighting the code using the mouse and then pressing **<Delete>**.*

Exercise 20 - Using Fields

Guidelines:

Fields are usually used to insert codes, which are updated to print current information.

Actions:

1. This exercise demonstrates how to insert fields into a document header. The fields will then be printed with the document. Open the document **Explanation**.

2. Select **File | Properties** and add your name to the document as **Author** and **Minutes** as the **Title**. Click **OK**.

3. Select **View | Header and Footer**. The **Header** appears, together with the **Header and Footer** toolbar.

continued over

Exercise 20 - Continued

4.   In the **Header** (with the cursor at the left margin), select **Insert | Field**.

5.   From the **Categories**, select **Document Information** and then select **Author** from **Field names**. Click **OK**.

6.   Tab to the centre. The **Header and Footer** toolbar can be used to add the name of the document as a code. Click **Insert AutoText** and select **Filename** from the list.

7.   Click the **Switch between Header and Footer** button, [icon].

8.   At the left of the **Footer**, insert the time by clicking the **Insert Time** button, [icon].

9.   Tab to the centre of the **Footer** and type **Page** followed by a space. Click the **Insert Page Number** button, [icon].

Note: *To stop a page number appearing on the first page of a document, you must use the command **Insert | Page Numbers** rather than the button and remove the check from **Show number on first page**.*

10.   Tab to the right of the **Footer** and click the **Insert Date** button, [icon], to insert the current date as a field.

11.   Close the **Footer** using the **Close** button, or by double clicking on a blank area of the screen.

12.   Print a copy of the document.

13.   Save the document as **Codes** and close it.

14.   Open **Introduction**.

15.   Add the **Date**, **Time** and **Filename** to the **Footer**.

16.   Print a copy of the document and close it <u>without</u> saving.

17.   Open **Codes**.

18.   Print the document again.

19.   Look at the time in the **Footer**. It shows the time the document was printed.

20.   Close the document <u>without</u> saving.

Exercise 21 - Working with Fields

Guidelines:

Fields can be used as a basis for a set document, where fields are given descriptive names and are then replaced at a later stage with the appropriate text.

Actions:

1. Open the document **Attendance**.

2. Ensure **Field codes** is checked, to view the fields that are in the document.

3. To move to the first field code and replace the contents, press **<F11>**. The cursor moves into the first field which is **{TIME \@"dd/MM/yy"}**.

4. Enter today's date. Press **<F11>** to move to the next field, **{Name}**.

5. Type **Mr Barker** to replace the field.

6. Press **<F11>** to move to the next field and enter **Dog Handler**.

Note: *Use **<F11>** or **<Alt F1>** to move from field to field. To move backwards, use* **<Shift F11>**.

7. Move to the next field and enter the interview date as next **Tuesday**.

8. In the next field, enter **2pm** for the time.

9. Enter **references** in the next field.

10. Print a copy of the letter.

11. Close the document <u>without</u> saving.

Exercise 22 - Updating Fields

Guidelines:

Fields containing information that changes, for example the time, can be updated to give new results by using the **<F9>** function key. Most fields are updated indirectly when printing or merging.

Actions:

1. Open the document **Tempus fugit**.

2. Make sure **Field codes** is checked and press **<Alt F9>** to view the actual times.

3. To update a single field, the cursor must be within the field. Position the cursor inside the **1:39:20** in the first line.

4. Press **<F9>** to update the time.

5. Try this again using the time on the second line.

6. Sometimes fields may not require updating. In order to keep a specific result, the **Lock Field** key **<Ctrl F11>** is used. Try updating the time on the third line. This time has been locked; the time is fixed and will not be updated.

Note: *To unlock a locked field press <**Ctrl Shift F11**> the **Unlock Field** key.*

7. Highlight the time in line **4**. **Lock** the field.

8. Try updating the field using **<F9>**.

9. With the cursor still in the line 4 time field, press **<Ctrl Shift F11>**. Now try updating the field using **<F9>**.

10. Wait two minutes, (to let the current time advance), note the time values then press the **Print Preview** button, . All the times except line 3 are updated.

11. Click **Close** to return to **Normal** view.

12. Close the document <u>without</u> saving.

Note: *To make sure that all fields are updated when printed, select **Tools | Options | Print** and check the **Update fields** box.*

Exercise 23 - Protecting Files

Guidelines:

Files can be protected by making them **Read-only**, so that they cannot be mistakenly changed. This means that any amendments to the file must be saved under a different name. If you try to save a **Read-only** file, a prompt will appear and you will have to change the file name before the process can be completed.

Actions:

1. Display the **Folders** on your computer and select the **Unit 1 Word XP Data** folder, a subfolder of the **Unit 1 Windows XP Data** folder, to display the files within it.

2. Right click on the file **Discovery**.

3. Click **Properties** to display the **Properties** dialog box.

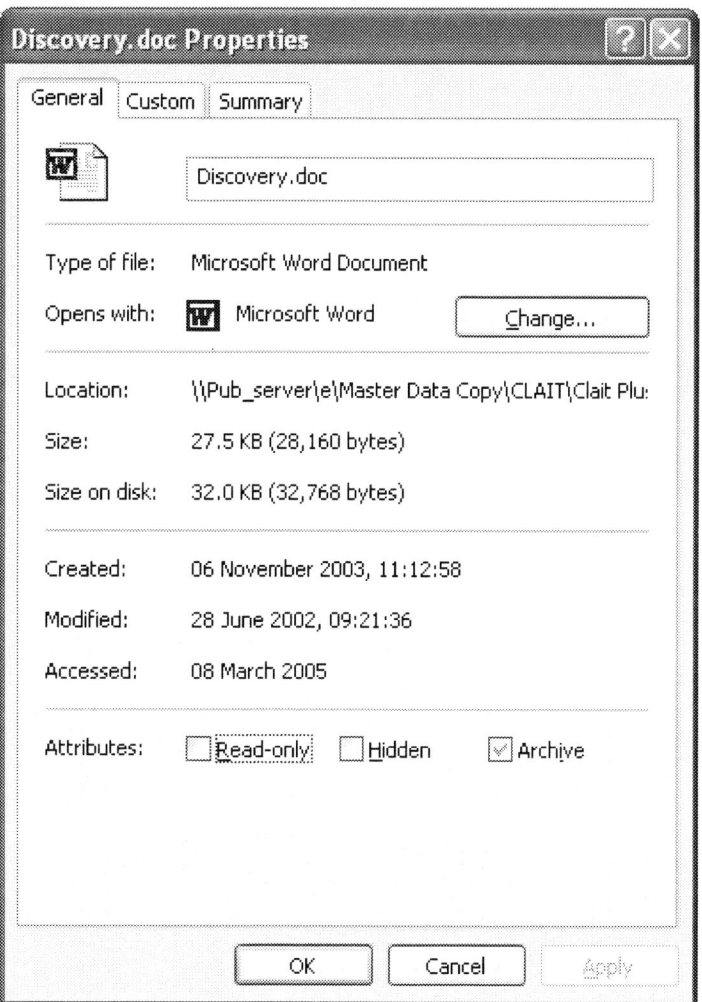

continued over

Exercise 23 - Continued

4. Click on the check box next to the **Read-only** attribute.

5. Click **OK** and close **Folder View**.

6. With *Word* open, open the document **Discovery**.

7. Add your name to the end of the document and click 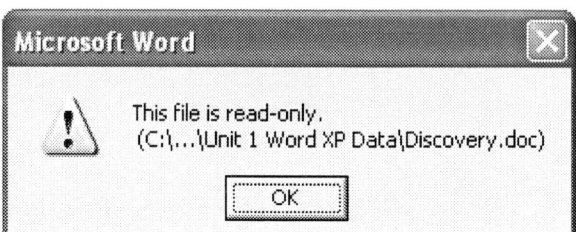. Notice that the **Save As** dialog box is displayed, rather than the document being saved automatically.

8. Click **Save** to save the document with the same name and the following prompt appears:

9. Click **OK** and amend the **File name** to **Discovery2**.

10. Now click **Save** again and the document is saved.

*Note: **Discovery2** does not have the **Read-only** attribute applied.*

11. Close the document.

12. Leave the *Word* application open.

Exercise 24 - Revision

1.   Open the document **Desiderata** from the **Unit 1 Word XP Data** folder.

2.   Insert the date as a field (use English date format) above the first line of the poem.

3.   Use **Cut** and **Paste** to place the lines of poetry in alphabetical order.

4.   What is the last item of the document in the new order?

5.   Adjust spacing if necessary.

6.   At the bottom of the document, type **These 19 points have been sorted alphabetically by** and enter your name.

7.   Check the document for spelling and grammatical errors.

8.   Print the document.

9.   Close it <u>without</u> saving.

Note: Check the Answers section at the back of the guide.

Section 3

Work with Tabular Data

By the end of this Section you should be able to:

Set and Align Tabs

Create a Table

Enter Text

Move and Resize a Table

Select Cells

Delete a Table

Change Column Width and Row Height

Merge, Split, Insert and Delete Cells

Insert Rows and Columns

Apply Gridlines, Borders and Shading

Exercise 25 - Tabs

Guidelines:

Tabs are a precise measurement for aligning vertical rows of text in a document and are set by default every 1.27cm. New tab settings will only apply to text that has been selected, or is yet to be typed. Tab settings are displayed on the ruler.

Actions:

1. Start a new document.

2. Select **Format | Tabs** to display the **Tabs** dialog box.

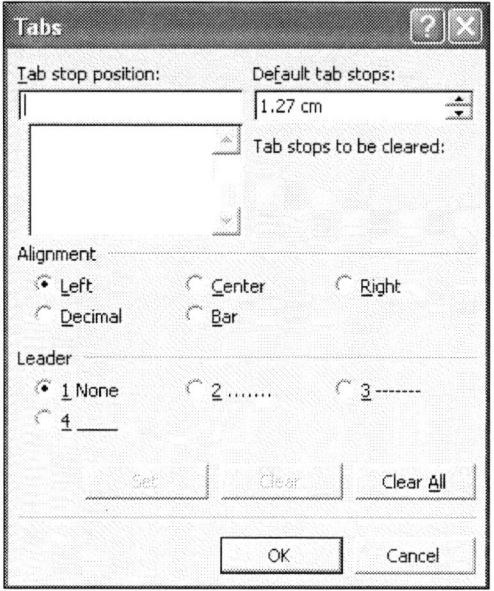

3. Enter **1cm** in the **Tab stop position** box. Check the **Alignment** is **Left** and the **Leader** is **None**. Click on **Set** to set the first tab.

4. Now enter **10** in the **Tab stop position** box, (**cm** is assumed if omitted). Click **Set**, then click **OK**.

5. Notice **L** markers have appeared on the ruler, these indicate the chosen settings. Press the **<Tab>** key before typing the word **Salesperson** and press <Tab> again to move to the next tab setting. Type **Sales** and press **<Enter>** to move to the next line. Enter the following information using the same method.

J Heslop	126.56
M Fisher	56
K Lowe	340.75
D Green	9.5
S Evans	1200
A Hargreaves	50.98

continued over

Exercise 25 - Continued

6.   Save the document as **Tabs** and print a copy.

*Note: To quickly set **Tabs**, click on the required position on the ruler. A tab symbol will appear where it is set.*

7.   Now select the entire document and clear the tab settings, using **Format | Tabs | Clear All** and **OK**.

8.   With the entire document selected use the mouse and click on the ruler approximately at **0.5cm** and **7cm** to set tabs.

*Note: Additional **Tab Stops** can be set by clicking on the required position on the ruler.*

9.   Print a copy of the document and close it <u>without</u> saving the changes.

10.   Open the file **Contents List**. Select the whole document and use the **Format | Tabs** command to display the **Tabs** dialog box.

11.   The two columns are too far apart. Before the tabs can be changed, select **Clear All** to remove the original tabs.

Note: Tabs can be removed by clicking on them and dragging the tab markers down, off the ruler.

12.   Set a new tab by entering **4cm** in the **Tab stop position** box. Click on **Set**.

13.   Repeat this for a tab at **11cm**. Click **OK**. View the changes.

*Note: **Tab Positions** can be changed by clicking and dragging the tab along the ruler to the required position.*

14.   With the document still selected, click on the left tab marker at **4cm** on the ruler and drag to **5cm**. Release the mouse button. The first column will move.

15.   Click on the first tab marker and drag it down off the ruler. The text automatically shifts to the next tab marker.

16.   Create a new tab stop at **3cm**.

17.   Practise using the mouse and ruler to move and remove tab markers.

18.   Close the document <u>without</u> saving, to remove the most recent tab settings.

Exercise 26 - Tab Alignment

Guidelines:

Left, Centre, Right and Decimal tabs are regularly used in word processing. Each of these determines how text is aligned at a particular tab stop position. Decimal tabs align numbers by their decimal points.

Actions:

1. Open the document **Tabs**. Select the entire document and move the tab positions to **4cm** and **11cm**.

2. Select **Format | Tabs** and from the dialog box, select the **Tab stop position** at **4cm**. Notice it is left aligned.

3. Click on **Right** from the **Alignment** options. Click **Set**.

4. Repeat this procedure for the tab at **11cm**, but make it **Centre** aligned.

5. Click **Set**. Click **OK** and observe the effect of the new tab alignment.

6. Select the whole document again and experiment by changing the tabs into right, left and centre tabs.

7. Close the document <u>without</u> saving and start a new one.

Note: Tabs can be set directly from the ruler by clicking on the left end of it, ⌊L⌋. The tabs alternate between ⌊L⌋, ⌊⊥⌋, ⌊⌐⌋, ⌊⊥⌋, ⌊I⌋, ▽ and ⌄ (Left, Centre, Right, Decimal, Bar, First Line Indent, Hanging Indent). Click on the ruler to place a tab stop of the current type at the position required.

8. Create a left tab approximately at **4cm** by clicking on the number **4** on the ruler.

9. Under this tab make a list, down the page, of the following numbers, making sure **<Tab>** is pressed before entering the number: **2.3**, **45**, **3.897**, **4567.99**, **234.01**, **6.8733**.

10. Select all the text and remove the old tab by clicking and dragging it down off the ruler.

11. Change the tab setting to **Decimal** by clicking on ⌊L⌋ at the left end of the ruler until ⌊⊥⌋ appears. With all of the text still selected, click on the number **5** on the ruler.

12. All the numbers should be lined up around their decimal points.

13. Close the document, <u>without</u> saving.

Note: To change the type of an existing tab stop, the existing tab must be **removed** before it is **replaced** with one of the required type.

Exercise 27 - Tables

Guidelines:

The table feature makes it easy to create documents, such as invoices, that have a tabular format. Tables provide a more effective way of presenting tabular data than tabs and allow that data to be manipulated more easily. Tables consist of rows, running from top to bottom and columns running from left to right, to create cells as in spreadsheets.

Actions:

1.   Start a new document.

2.   To create a table with 4 rows and 4 columns, select **Table | Insert | Table**.

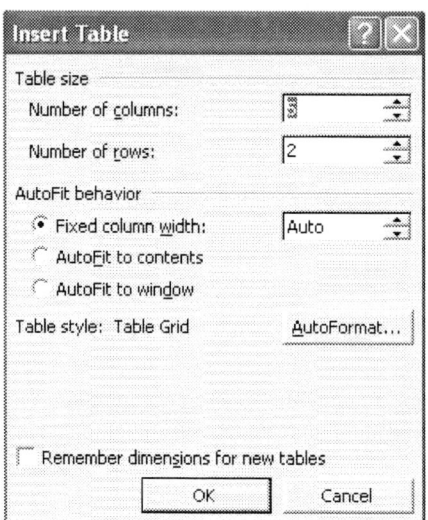

3.   When the **Insert Table** dialog box appears, enter **4** in the **Number of columns** box and enter **4** in the **Number of rows** box (these numbers can be typed in, or the arrows can be clicked to change them).

4.   Click **OK** to create the table.

Note: *Alternatively, a table can be created using the **Insert Table** button,* *Click and drag the required number of cells on the grid.*

5.   Leave the document open for the next exercise.

Exercise 28 - Entering Text

Guidelines:

Once a table has been created, it is simple to enter text and move around within it. It is probably easier to type the text into the table first and then to format it, i.e. correct column widths, etc.

Actions:

1. Using the table created in the previous exercise, move to the first cell.

*Note: Use **<Tab>** to move forward in a table and **<Shift Tab>** to move backwards. The cursor can also be positioned in the required cell by clicking. When entering text, do not use **<Enter>** unless a new line is required within the same cell, e.g. as in an address.*

2. Enter the following text into the table:

Company	Share Price	Sector	Type of Business
Global	1240	Chemicals	PetroChemicals
Biro Bank	300	Banking	Corporate Finance
Sparkys	130	Stores	Electrical Retailer

3. Save the document as **Table**.

4. Close the document.

Exercise 29 - Move or Resize a Table

Guidelines:

Once a table has been created, it can be moved to a different position on the page and made larger or smaller.

Actions:

1.   Open the document **Station** and ensure **Print Layout** view is displayed by selecting **View | Print Layout**.

2.   Rest the mouse on the table until the **Table Move Handle**, ⊞, appears at the top left corner of the table.

3.   Now move the mouse over the **Table Move Handle** until a four-headed arrow appears, as in the diagram below.

4.   Click and drag the mouse downward to move the table.

5.   Rest the mouse on the table until the **Table Resize Handle**, □, appears at the bottom right corner of the table.

6.   Now move the mouse over the **Table Resize Handle** until a double headed arrow appears, as in the diagram below.

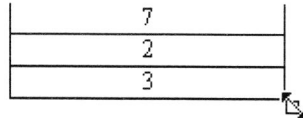

7.   Drag the mouse to the left until the table is about half its original width.

8.   Now use the **Table Resize Handle** to return the table to its original state.

9.   Move the table to the top of the page.

10.   Close the document <u>without</u> saving any changes.

Exercise 30 - Selecting Cells

Guidelines:

> To act on a group of cells they must be selected first, just as a block of text must be selected before it is formatted. Selection arrows are used to select a cell, or group of cells.

Actions:

1. In a new document, create a table with **5** columns and **5** rows.

2. Ensure **Print Layout View** is selected so the **Table Move Handle** will be displayed.

3. Select the first cell by moving inside its left edge and clicking the left mouse button when the ◢ arrow is displayed.

4. Move the mouse down and click again to select the other cells in the first column in turn.

5. Move the mouse near to the top edge of the second column, until the ↓ selection arrow is displayed.

6. Click once to select the column.

7. Select the entire second row by clicking once when the ⬉ selection arrow is displayed at the left edge of the table.

8. Select the nine cells in the middle of the table by clicking and dragging.

9. To select the entire table, move the mouse over the **Table Move Handle** and click once.

10. Close the document <u>without</u> saving.

*Note: Alternatively, to select a row or column, position the cursor within the row/column then use **Table | Select | Row** or **Table | Select | Column**. **Table | Select | Table** will select the entire table.*

Exercise 31 - Deleting a Table

Guidelines:

Tables can easily be deleted, if necessary.

Actions:

1. Start a new document.

2. Click once on the **Insert Table** button, . Move the cursor across the cells until a **3 x 3** table is highlighted.

3. Click the mouse button to place the table on the document.

4. Make sure the cursor is flashing within the table, otherwise this deletion method will not work.

5. Select the table, either by using the **Table Move Handle**, or by selecting **Table | Select | Table**.

6. Once the table has been highlighted, select **Table | Delete | Table**. The table should now be deleted.

Note: *To delete the contents of a table, first select the contents to be deleted, then press **<Delete>**.*

7. Close the document <u>without</u> saving.

Exercise 32 - Changing Column Width/Row Height

Guidelines:

When creating columns of text or figures, tables have an advantage over tab stops. The width of columns and height of rows can be changed directly on the table. The total width of a table is restricted by the space available between the margins. Reduce the width of large columns before widening others.

Actions:

1. Open the document **Table** and select **View | Ruler** to display the ruler if it is not already on the screen.

2. Move the cursor into the table. When inside the table the ruler shows the table column divides as symbols within the ruler.

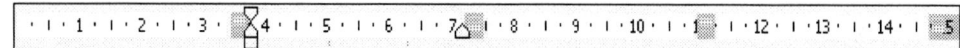

3. A column width is changed by clicking on the divide between two columns in the table, the cursor changes to a double-headed arrow, ╫ and then dragging to a new position before releasing the mouse button. Move the column divide between the first and second column left to about 2 cm.

Note: Row height can be changed similarly, using the boundary between the rows.

4. Column width can also be changed from within the ruler. First, move the mouse over the border between the second and third columns (a grey square). A double-headed arrow appears when the mouse pointer is over the division.

5. Click and drag to the left until **Share Price** fits on two lines.

6. Change the height of the rows by selecting **Table | Select | Table**, then **Table | Table Properties** and the **Row** tab. Check the **Specify height** option and increase the height to **1 cm**, then click **OK**.

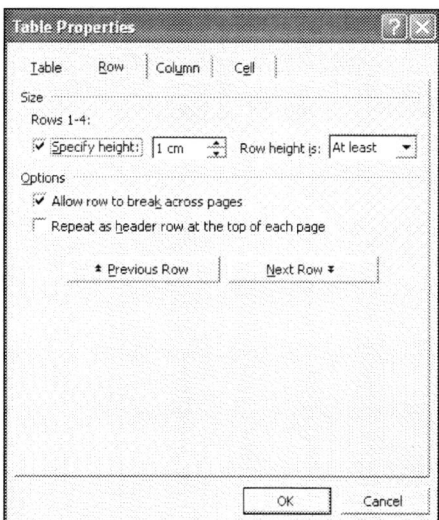

continued over

Exercise 32 - Continued

7.   To change the vertical alignment of the text, with the table still selected, open the **Table Properties** dialog box again.

8.   Click the **Cell** tab to display the following alignment options. Under **Vertical Alignment** are the three options, **Top**, **Center** and **Bottom**.

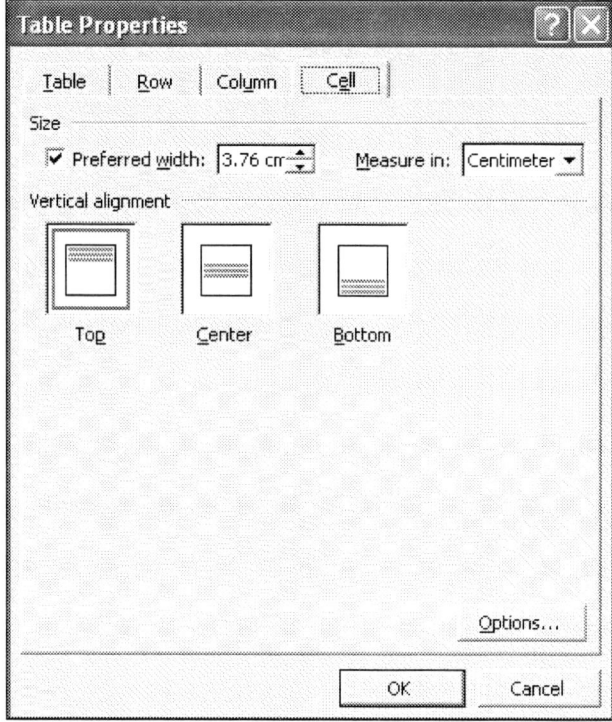

9.   Select the **Center** option then click **OK**. All of the text is now centred vertically in each cell of the table.

10.   To change the horizontal alignment of the table on the page, open the **Table Properties** dialog box again with the table still selected.

11.   Click the **Table** tab and under the **Alignment** heading, select the **Center** option.

12.   Click **OK** and the table will be centred between the left and right margins.

13.   To change the horizontal alignment of text within cells, first click and drag to select the text in the required cells rather than the table itself.

14.   Any of the available formatting tools may now be applied to the selected text. Click the **Center** button, on the **Formatting** toolbar to centre the selected text horizontally within the cell.

15.   Save the document as **Table2** and close it.

Exercise 33 - Merging and Splitting Cells

Guidelines:

Cells in a table can be merged or split. To merge cells means to join two or more cells together to make one large cell. To split cells means to divide a cell into two or more cells.

Actions:

1. In a new document, create a table with **5** columns and **10** rows.

2. Move to the second cell on the top line, select that cell and the cell to the right of it. Select **Table | Merge Cells**. The cells are merged. Click away to view.

Note: The **Merge Cells** button, 🖽, on the **Tables and Borders** toolbar can also be used.

3. Merge the two cells at the right of the top row and all of the cells on the second row.

4. Merge cells **1** and **2** on rows **3** to **9**. This must be done one row at a time.

5. Merge cells **1** to **4** on the bottom row. Your employer wants you to keep a record of daily sales to keep in your Personal Development folder. Enter text into the table until it matches the diagram below.

Date	Name		Department	
Product		Price	Quantity	Total Price
Grand Total				

6. Your employer now decides that product reference numbers should be added to the table. Position the cursor in the cell containing **Product** and select **Table | Split Cells**. Make sure **2** columns and **1** row are selected from the **Split Cells** dialog box and click **OK**.

7. Enter **Ref.** in the cell to the right of **Product** and split the cells in the six rows below (use the **Split Cells** button, 🖽, on the **Tables and Borders** toolbar).

Note: Cells that have not been merged can still be split.

8. Save the document as **Daily Sales** and close it.

Exercise 34 - Inserting and Deleting Cells

Guidelines:

Once a table has been created, cells can be added or deleted at any time.

Actions:

1. Open **Table2**.

2. Click in the first cell on the top row and select **Table | Insert | Cells** to display the **Insert Cells** dialog box.

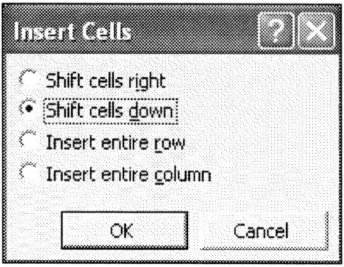

3. To insert a cell to the left of the current one, select **Shift Cells Right** and click **OK**.

4. The table will now be out of alignment. It is more usual to insert an entire row/column (see the following exercise), or split cells. Delete the cell by first making sure it is selected, then select **Table | Delete | Cells**.

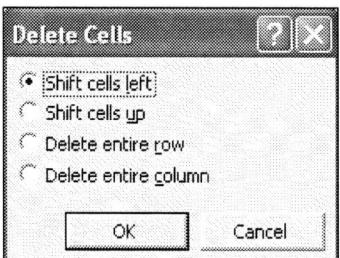

5. Select **Shift Cells Left**.

6. Click **OK** to delete the cell.

Note: The columns may not be aligned after these steps and may need adjusting.

7. Close the table <u>without</u> saving any changes.

Exercise 35 - Inserting Rows and Columns

Guidelines:

The size of a table can be increased by adding rows and columns above or below, or to the left or right of existing rows and columns.

Actions:

1. Use the document **Table**. Select the first column and click the **Insert Columns** button, ⬒. A column is inserted to the left of the original.

2. Now select the new column and select **Table | Insert | Columns to the Right**. A column appears to the right of the selected column.

3. Select the first row, by clicking outside the table to the left of the first cell of the row, then click the **Insert Rows** button, ⬓. A row is inserted above the selected row.

4. With the new row selected, select **Table | Insert | Rows Below**. A row is inserted underneath the selected row.

5. With the newest row selected, right click on the selection to display a shortcut menu.

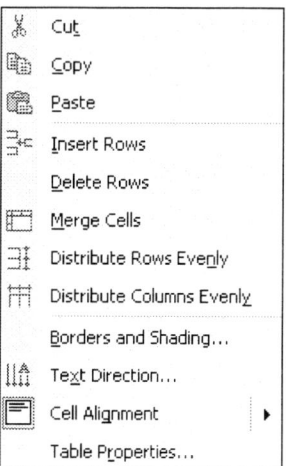

6. Select **Insert Rows** from the menu to insert a row above the current row.

7. Select the column at the right of the table and right click on a part of the selection to display a shortcut menu.

8. Select **Insert Columns** to insert a column to the left of the current column.

9. Close **Table** <u>without</u> saving.

Exercise 36 - Gridlines and Borders

Guidelines:

Borders can be added to individual cells, to a range of cells, or to a whole table. Gridlines are non-printing guides surrounding cells; however, a **Grid Border** can be applied to a table and follows the gridlines.

Actions:

1.   Open the document **Table2**. Select the table, then select **Format | Borders and Shading** to display the following dialog box.

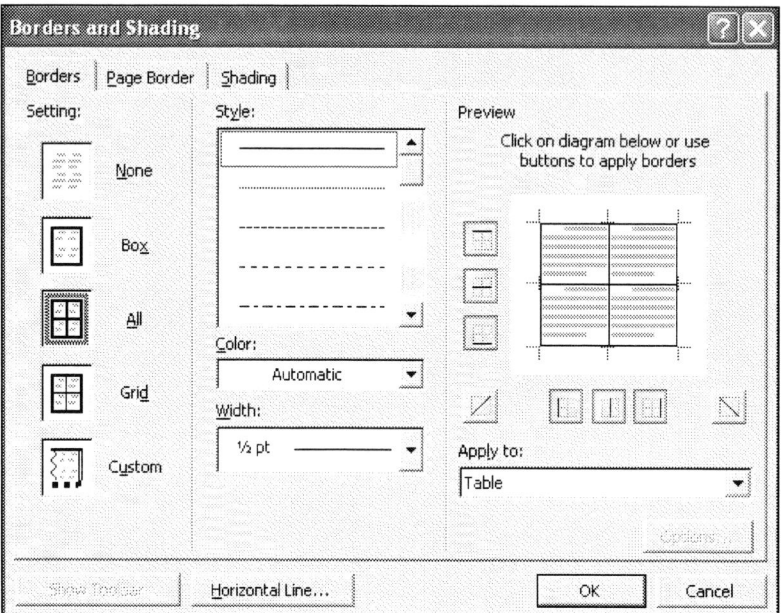

2.   To remove the borders and see the **Gridlines**, select **None** from the **Setting** area and click **OK**. These lines are there to act as a guide.

3.   Resize the third column to fit the text, then select the table again.

4.   Select **Table | Hide Gridlines**. This is how the table would appear, were it to be printed now. Replace the **Gridlines** by selecting **Table | Show Gridlines**.

5.   Select the top row of the table, then display the **Borders and Shading** dialog box again.

6.   This time, select **Box** from the **Settings** area (notice the **Preview Apply to** area shows **Cell**). Click **OK**.

Note: The buttons in the Preview area can be used to apply borders.

7.   Practise adding different borders, then close the document <u>without</u> saving.

Exercise 37 - Shading

Guidelines:

Shading can be used to enhance the appearance of a table or to draw attention to a particular cell. A few minutes spent removing lines, merging and splitting cells or adding some shading, can enhance the appearance of a document drastically.

Actions:

1. Open the document **Personnel**.

2. Select the **Date** cell and select **Format | Borders and Shading**, making sure the **Shading** tab is selected.

3. Choose the **Gray-15% Fill** colour (as shown below).

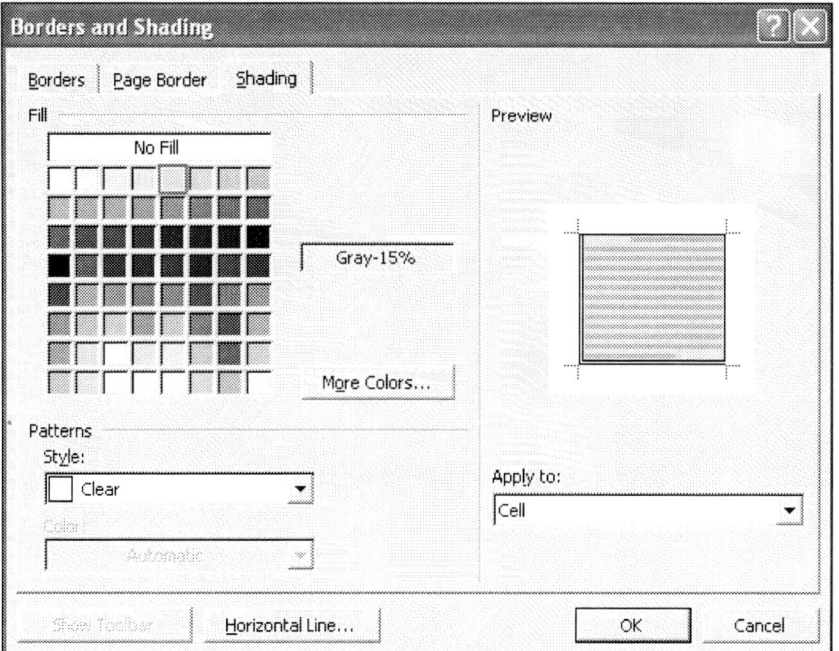

4. Click **OK**. Deselect the cell to see the effect of the shading.

5. Shade the top row with **Gray-15%**.

6. Select the rest of the table (click and drag down the left side) and shade it with one of the pale colours from the bottom row of the **Shading** palette.

7. Experiment further with shading.

8. Close the document <u>without</u> saving.

Exercise 38 - Revision

1. Start a new document.

2. Create a new table to match the table below, an invoice.

Invoice				
Ref No	Description	Qty	Price	Total
Subtotal				
VAT				
Total				

3. Save the document as **InvoiceTable** and close it.

4. Start a second new document.

5. Create the following table with the text, lines and shading.

Date		Order Form		Terms	
	Title	**Type**	**Licence Number**		**Price**
Total					

6. Save the document as **Orders**.

7. Print a copy of the table.

8. Close the document.

Section 4

Mail Merge

By the end of this Section you should be able to:

Create a Main Document

Create a Data Source

nsert Merge Codes

Format a Mail Merge Document

Protect a Main Document

Create a Mail Merge Query

Perform Mail Merge

Exercise 39 - Mail Merge

Guidelines:

The **mail merge** feature is used to combine a **main document** (a letter, for example), with a separate list - the **data source** (names and addresses, for example), into one document. These two files, when merged, create a personalised copy of the document for everyone on the list. Mailing labels to the same group of people can be created, if required, using the same technique.

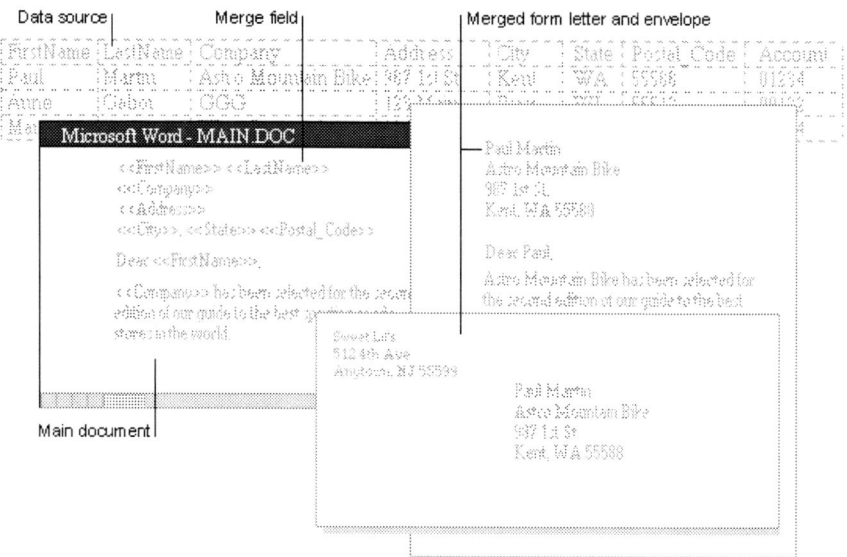

Two important terms that are used with merging are **field** and **record**. The following example shows fields (columns - **Surname**, **First name**, **Street**, **Town**, **County**) and records (rows - information for each person):

Surname	First name	Street	Town	County
Chapman	Ian	7 The Avenue	Boldon	Tyne & Wear
Peagram	Norma	5 St Georges	Morpeth	Northumberland

A **data source** is a document containing all the records used in a merged document in table format. These documents need a great deal of planning as they can be used for various applications.

It is best to break the information into as many fields as possible. For example, **Name** could be a field, but, **Surname**, **First Name** and **Initial** would be more useful, depending on requirements. Paul French entered in one field cannot be used in a merged document as P French, Paul, Mr French or Mr P French. Every record must have exactly the same number of fields, so some fields may have to be left blank.

Data source files are used many times. As situations change, it will be necessary to add new records, change records and delete records. These changes can be made using the standard editing techniques.

Exercise 40 - Creating a Main Document

Guidelines:

Word XP gives a great deal of assistance to the mail merge process in the form of a **Mail Merge** task pane. This takes a user through the six steps necessary to complete the task with lots of prompts for the required information.

The first part of the mail merge process is to define and select the type of main document. A main document can take a range of formats, such as form letters, e-mail messages, mailing labels, envelopes or catalogues.

Actions:

1. In a new document, start the **Mail Merge** task pane using **Tools | Letters and Mailings | Mail Merge Wizard**.

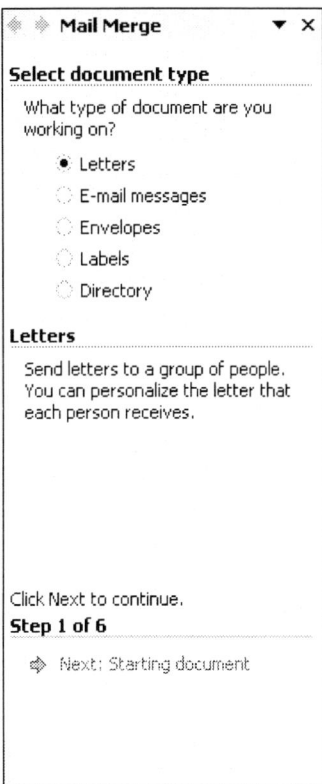

Note: *The first step of the task pane is displayed showing **Step 1 of 6**. You can move forwards and backwards through the 6 steps using the **Next** and **Previous** navigation controls at the bottom of the pane.*

2. Select the document type options in turn and read the descriptive text for each.

continued over

Exercise 40 - Continued

3.   Make sure **Letters** is selected from **Select document type** and click **Next: Starting document** at the bottom of the pane.

4.   Step **2** defines where the main document will be found. This could be based on an existing template or document but in this exercise we will use the current new document. Make sure that is the selected option.

5.   Enter the current date in the blank document on the left, using **Insert | Date and Time**. From the **Available formats**, select the date in the format **18 March 2005** and click **OK**.

6.   Add 2 blank lines. Type the following paragraph.

Dear

The "Using the Internet for Business" conference is only a few weeks away. I look forward to your call to reserve your place. Delegates are limited to 1500, so please hurry.

Sincerely

Ms W W Webb

Note: *The main document could be left blank at this stage and entered later as part of step 4.*

7.   Save the document as **Main** in the **Unit 1 Word XP Data** folder.

8.   Leave it open for the next exercise.

Exercise 41 - Creating a Data Source

A data source can be used with any number of main documents, so it must be well planned, but not all of the fields or records in the data source have to be used with every document. The data source can be created before or after the main document and can be accessed at any time once created.

Actions:

1.   Click **Next: Select Recipients** at the bottom of the task pane.

2.   At step **3**, select to **Type a new list** and click on .

Select recipients

- Use an existing list
- Select from Outlook contacts
- ● Type a new list

Type a new list

Type the names and addresses of recipients.

Create...

Create new recipient list

Note: *A data source may already exist. If this is the case, it can be opened to use with the main document by selecting **Use an existing list** from the task pane.*

3.   The **New Address List** dialog box appears. This will be used to create the mailing list.

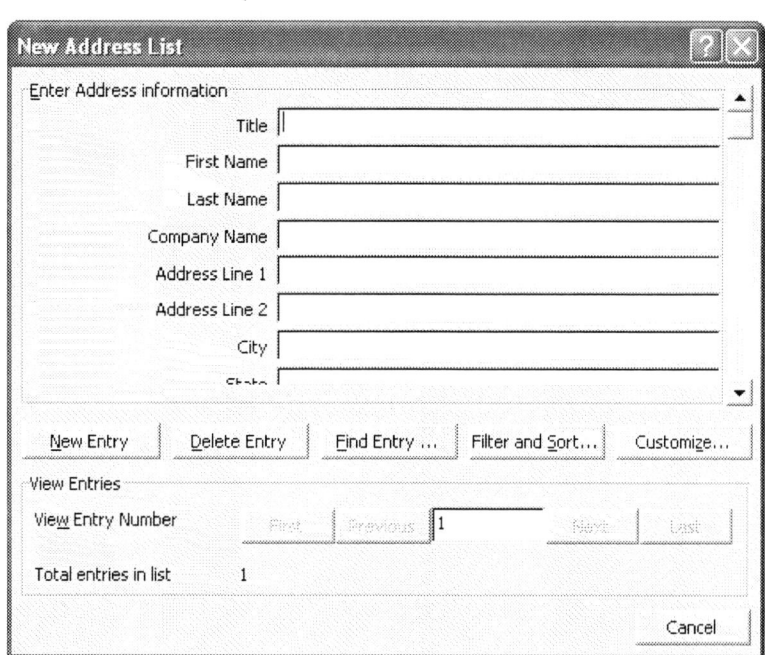

continued over

Exercise 41 - Continued

4.   Click the **Customize** button to edit the field names.

5.   Remove field names so that only **Title**, **Last Name**, **Company Name**, **Address Line 1**, **Address Line 2** and **City** remain. Do this by clicking on the field name that is not needed and then **Delete**, selecting **Yes** at the prompt.

6.   Add **Initial** by clicking **Add**. Type **Initial** into the box provided.

7.   Click **OK** to add the field then move it to the appropriate place in the list above **Last Name** using the **Move Up** button.

8.   Click **OK** to return to the **New Address List** dialog box.

9.   Use the <**Tab**> key to move from field to field, entering your own details and those of 3 other people (fictitious if necessary).

10.   Select **New Entry** after each record. Click on **Close** to end.

11.   When the **Save Address List** dialog box appears, change the default location of **My Data Sources** to the **Unit 1 Word XP Data** folder where the other data files are stored, and save it a with the **File name** of **Data**.

12.   The **Mail Merge Recipients** dialog box appears. Records can be sorted, filtered, de-selected (by removing the tick on the left) and amended from this screen.

Note: *To add or remove records, first click **Edit** with any record highlighted. De-selected records will not appear in the mail merge but are not removed from the source.*

13.   Click **OK** to close it without making any changes.

Note: *The **Mail Merge Recipients** button,* *can be used to display this dialog box at any time to maintain the source records or change the selection.*

14.   Leave the **Main** document open for the next exercise.

Exercise 42 - Adding Merge Codes

Guidelines:

Now that the data source fields (merge codes) have been defined, they can be incorporated into the main document where required. Use the **Mail Merge** task pane and the **Mail Merge** toolbar to help. When the merge process is run, these fields will be replaced by the actual data from the source records. The main document can also be formatted at this stage.

Actions:

1. Click **Next: Write your letter** at the bottom of the task pane to move to step **4**. Notice that the **Mail Merge** toolbar is displayed.

2. With the **Main** document on the screen, add 2 blank lines at the top.

3. Place the cursor at the top of the document and click 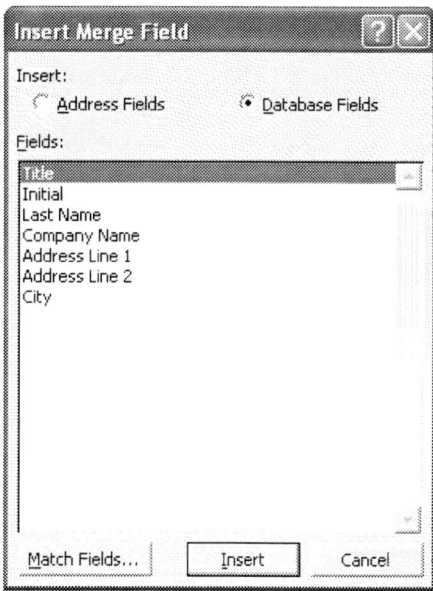 More items... from the **Mail Merge** task pane.

4. Select **Title** from the **Insert Merge Field** dialog box and click **Insert**.

5. Now insert **Initial**.

6. Insert all of the remaining fields, one after the other: **Last Name**, **Company Name**, **Address Line 1**, **Address Line 2** and **City**.

7. Close the dialog box.

continued over

Exercise 42 - Continued

8.   The fields have been inserted but they are in one continuous line. Add spaces after **Title** and **Initial**, and press **<Enter>** after each of the other fields, so that the text matches the diagram below.

«Title» «Initial» «Last_Name»
«Company_Name»
«Address_Line_1»
«Address_Line_2»
«City»

9.   After **Dear** in the main part of the document, insert a space.

10.   Use the **Insert Merge Fields** button, ▣, on the **Mail Merge** toolbar to display the **Insert Merge Field** dialog box.

11.   Insert the **Title** field followed by **Last Name** then close the dialog box.

12.   In the document, insert a space between the **Title** and **Last_Name** fields.

Note: *To format merged data, you must format the merge fields in the main document. The formatting in the data source isn't retained when merge fields are added to the document. Mail merge documents are formatted using the same techniques as for normal documents. See Exercises 53-59 for more information about finishing documents and ensuring consistency.*

13.   Select the whole document, then set the font as **Arial 11pt**.

Note: *A mail merge main document can be protected by making it read-only, to prevent any changes being made to it (see Exercise 23).*

14.   Save the document using the same name, **Main**.

Note: *To remove a data source associated with a main document, click **Main Document Setup** on the **Mail Merge** toolbar, select **Normal Word document** and click **OK**.*

15.   Leave the **Main** document open for the next exercise.

Exercise 43 - Merging

Guidelines:

The hardest part of mail merge is the creation of the main and data source documents. It is easy to merge the two files. The new merged file can be saved, although this is not essential as the two component files (main document and data source) are already saved separately. Be aware that saving a merged file containing many records can take up a lot of disk space.

Actions:

1. Click **Next: Preview your letters** on the task pane to move to step **5**. The main document (letter) is shown merged with the data fields from the first source data record.

2. Use the **Next Recipient** button, >> , in the task pane to move through the letters.

3. Click **Next: complete the merge**, and read the information in the task pane.

4. To print the merged letters, click Print... from the **Merge** area of the pane.

5. When the **Merge to Printer** dialog box appears, make sure **All** is selected.

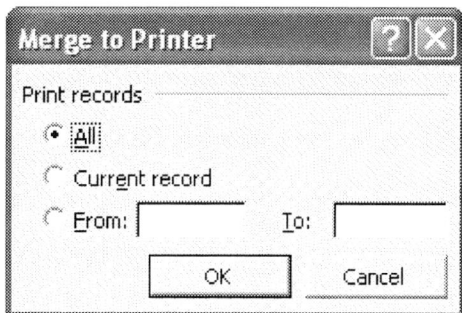

6. Click **OK**. Click **OK** again in the **Print** dialog box to print the merged letters.

7. To save the complete merged document, select **Edit individual letters** from the task pane.

8. With **All** selected in the **Merge to New Document** dialog box, click **OK**. A document is created with all the merged letters in it.

9. Save this document as **Letters2** and close it.

10. Close the **Main** document, <u>saving</u> the changes.

Exercise 44 - Performing Mail Merge Queries

Guidelines:

All records from a data source do not have to be used in each mail merge. The source may contain thousands of records for customers all over the country, but it may only be necessary to send letters to customers in London, for example. In these situations, a **Query** can be performed, to specify which records are to be included in the merge.

Actions:

1. Open the document **Conference**. This document has been saved as the main document of a mail merge, so a message may be displayed requiring you to find the data source.

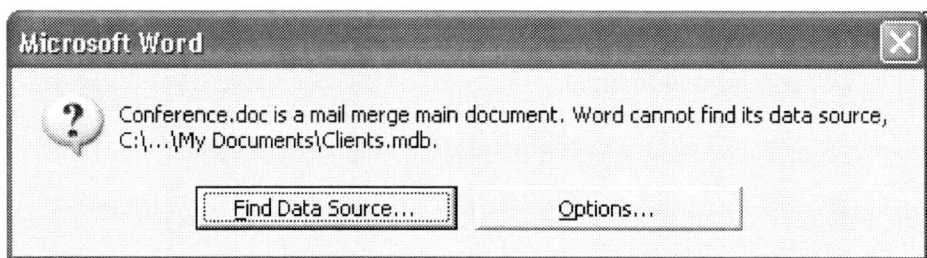

2. Click **Find Data Source** and locate the file **Clients.mdb** in the **Unit 1 Word XP Data** folder. Click **Open**.

3. If a message appears about the data being placed in the document, click **Yes** to continue.

4. Select **Tools | Letters and Mailings | Mail Merge Wizard** to view the **Mail Merge** task pane.

5. Select **Edit recipient list** on the **Mail Merge** task pane and widen the **Town** column in the dialog box by clicking and dragging the right edge of the heading until the whole contents can be seen.

6. Scroll down the list of records. There are 32 clients listed for a variety of different towns. By default the mail merge would produce a letter for each of the 32 records.

7. To print only letters to **Sunderland** addresses, click the **Town** drop down arrow and select **Advanced** from the list.

continued over

Exercise 44 - Continued

8.   In the **Filter and Sort** dialog box click on the **Field** drop down list and select **Town**. Make sure **Comparison** shows **Equal to** and enter **Sunderland** in **Compare to**.

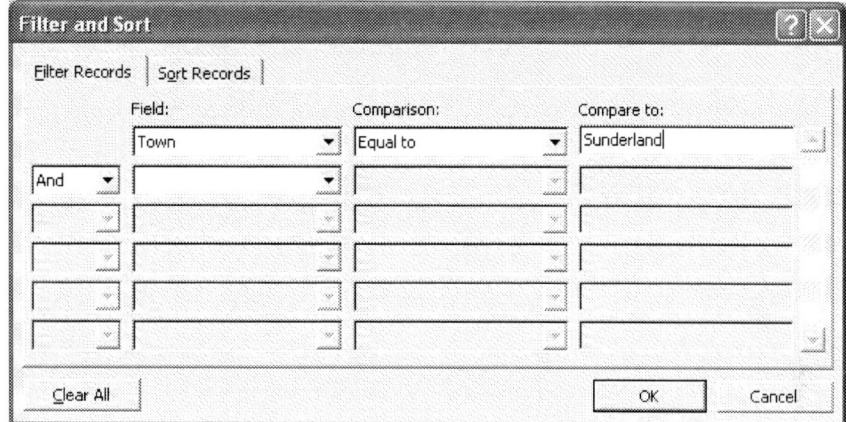

9.   Click **OK**. The **Mail Merge Recipients** dialog box is displayed again.

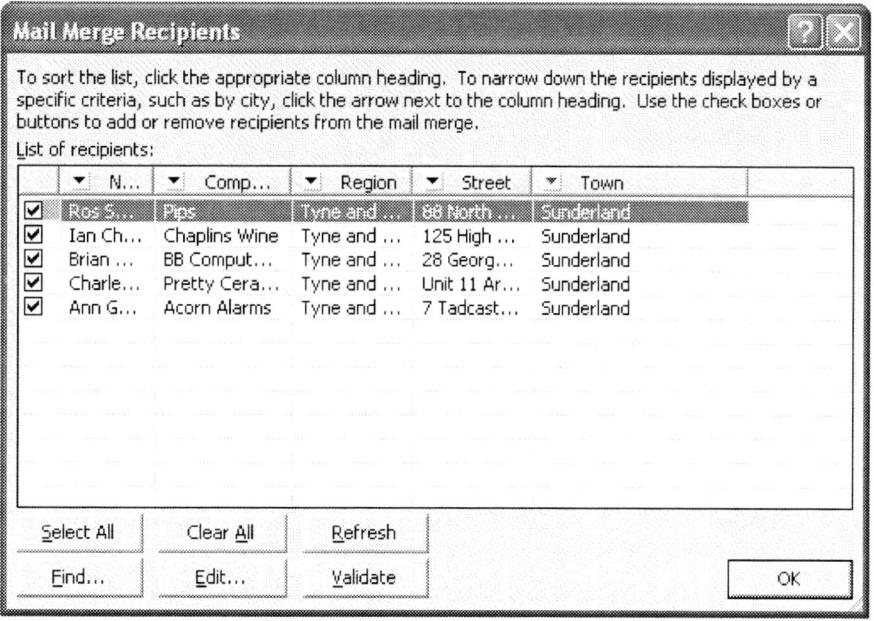

10. A query has been applied to the source data table and now only the five records for Sunderland are displayed. These are the only records that will be used in the mail merge. Click **OK** again.

11. Move to step 5 (the merge fields are already inserted) and preview each of the 5 letters in turn. They are all to Sunderland addresses.

12. Complete the merge and print the 5 letters.

13. Close **Conference** <u>without</u> saving.

Exercise 45 - Revision

1. Which two types of document/file are combined in a mail merge?

2. Open the document **Proposal**. This is attached to the source document **Clubmembers**.

3. At the top of the document, enter the merge codes as shown in the diagram below:

Cosmopolitan Cocktail Group
15-29 Riverside
Smalltown
New County

Wednesday, 20 April 2005

«Title» «First_Name» «Last_Name»
«Address_Line_1»
«Address_Line_2»
«City»

Dear «First_Name»,

At Cosmopolitan Cocktail Group, we are thinking of starting a weekly Ladies' Night at selected local clubs, from May. The proposed evening for this event is Thursday.

4. The mail merge is to be sent to females only (**Gender = F**). Filter the mail merge recipients accordingly.

5. Complete the merge to a new document.

6. How many letters are produced?

7. Save the merged file as **Cocktails** and close it.

8. Close any other documents <u>without</u> saving.

Note: *Check the Answers section at the back of the guide.*

Section 5

Integrate Documents

By the end of this Section you should be able to:

Create a Base Document

Import Data, Images and Charts

Edit and Format Objects

Print an Integrated Document

Exercise 46 - Creating the Base Document

Guidelines:

As the assessment for this unit, you will be required to create a document and import different types of file into it. This base document can be created from scratch, or created from an existing text or *Word* document. A draft text document is used for this exercise. It will form the basis of a brief report to a company director about sales performance.

Actions:

1. In *Word*, open the text file called **Draft Document**. As this is a text file rather than a *Word* document, you will need to view **All Documents** from **Files of type** in the **Open** dialog box.

2. Select **File | Save As** and select **Word Document** from **Save as type**.

3. Name the document **Integration**.

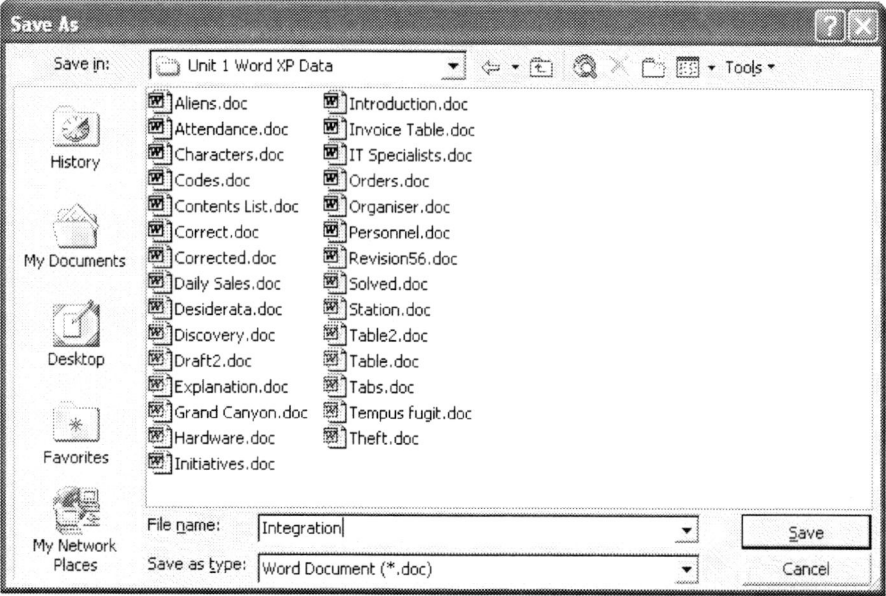

Some of the files shown above may be different if the Revision Exercises have not been completed

4. Save the document.

5. Spell check the document and correct any errors.

6. Centre the heading and make it bold.

7. Click ⊞ to save the changes to the document.

8. Leave the document **Integration** open for the next exercise.

Exercise 47 - Importing Objects

Guidelines:

Many different objects can be created within a document. Using this facility, objects from other applications on the computer can be inserted into the *Word* document.

Actions:

1. Use the document **Integration** for this exercise.

2. Position the cursor at the end of the first paragraph, ...**figures as below** and press <**Enter**> to move to the next line.

3. Select **Insert | Object** and the **Create from File** tab.

Note: If the object is not already created, select the **Create New** tab. Select the correct type of object, then click **OK**.

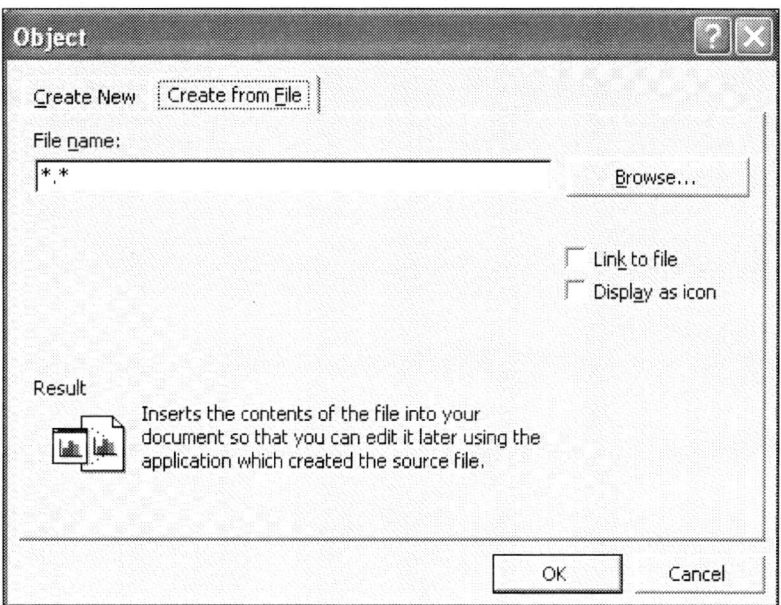

4. To insert an *Excel* spreadsheet file, click **Browse** at the right of the dialog box.

5. Locate the **Unit 1 Windows XP Data** folder using the **Look in** drop down list. Open the **Unit 1 Word XP Data** folder.

6. Select the **First half.xls** file.

continued over

Exercise 47 - Continued

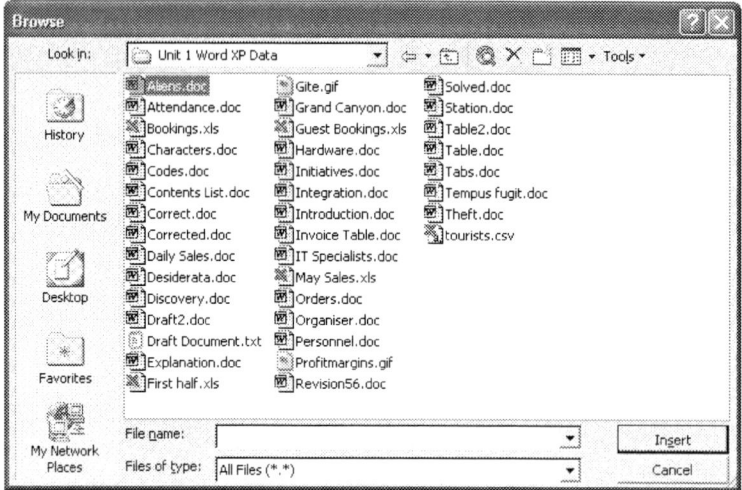

7. Click **Insert**.

8. In the **Object** dialog box, click **OK**.

9. The spreadsheet is imported, but it needs to be centred on the page. Click on the worksheet to select it.

*Note: If it appears as code, press <**Alt F9**> to show the data.*

10. Click the **Center** button, ⬚.

Note: You will probably have noticed that there is not sufficient space above and below the spreadsheet. This will be corrected in a later Section.

11. Save the changes to the document.

12. Data can also be imported in a universally accepted simple text format, with each field of data separated from the next by a 'delimiter', often a comma. If a comma is used, the file is known as **a 'Comma Separated Variable'** type with a **.csv** file extension. Start a new document.

13. Select **Insert | Object** and the **Create from File** tab. Click **Browse** and select the file **tourists.csv**.

14. Click **Insert** and then **OK**. Notice the difference from the imported spreadsheet in the **Integration** document - the columns aren't wide enough to display the data and there is no formatting.

15. This could be corrected by selecting the imported table and then double clicking on it. The columns could then be widened, etc. However, for now just close the document <u>without</u> saving.

16. Leave the document **Integration** open for the next exercise.

Exercise 48 - Importing an Image

Guidelines:

Pictures from existing files can be inserted into *Word*. This means that many more graphics can be used in a document than are available from **ClipArt**.

Actions:

1. Using the document **Integration**, as modified in the last exercise, position the cursor beneath the title and centre it.

2. Select **Insert | Picture | From File** to display the **Insert Picture** dialog box.

3. Make sure that **Look in** shows the location where the **Unit 1 Word XP Data** is stored and **Files of type** shows **All Pictures**.

4. Select the file named **Profitmargins.gif** and **Preview** from the **Views** button, a preview appears at the right of the dialog box.

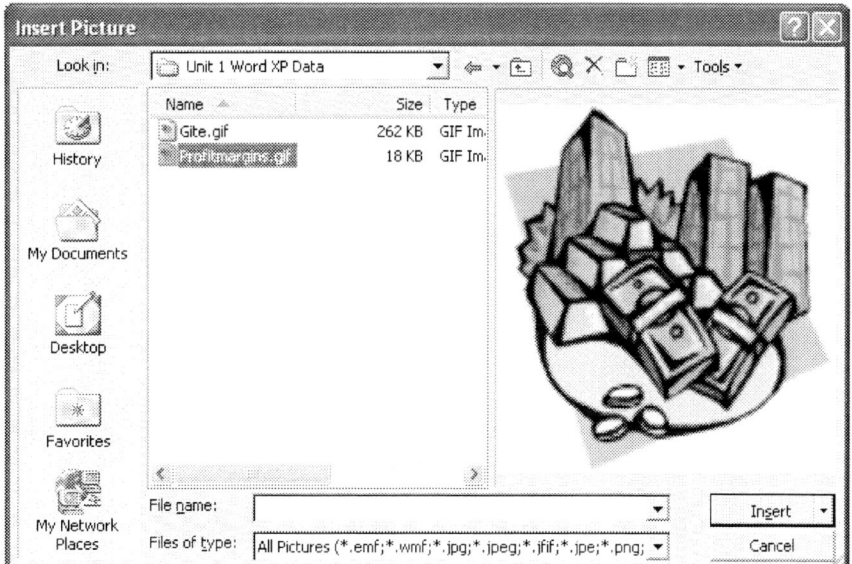

5. Click **Insert** to position the picture on the page.

6. The picture is too large. Click on it to select it.

7. It is important to maintain the proportions of pictures and other objects such as charts when resizing them. Using a corner handle, click and drag inwards to make the picture about half its original size.

8. Save the changes to the document.

9. Leave the document **Integration** open for the next exercise.

Exercise 49 - Importing a Chart

Guidelines:

A chart can be added to a document to display information professionally. This could be useful when producing a report containing figures, for example.

Actions:

1.   Use the document **Integration**, as modified in the last exercise. A chart is to be created to show the totals of the sales departments for May, the worst month for losses.

2.   Position the cursor after the text **...poor performance areas more clearly** and press <**Enter**>. Centre the cursor.

3.   Use the **Insert | Object** process described in **Exercise 42** to import the chart from the **May Sales** spreadsheet file within the **Unit 1 Word XP Data** folder.

Note: When the spreadsheet file being imported contains more than one worksheet, only the currently active sheet is retrieved, that is the sheet that was active when the spreadsheet file was last saved.

4.   The chart is imported into the document, but is a little too big. Select it and use a corner handle to reduce the size of the chart until it fits neatly between the margins.

Note: It is important to maintain the integrity of the data when resizing the chart – make sure it can still be read.

5.   Make sure that **Print Layout View** is active.

6.   Do not worry if the chart is on a second page. Save the changes to the document.

7.   Leave the document **Integration** open for the next exercise.

*Note: An alternative method of importing the chart would be to open the **May Sales** spreadsheet in Excel, select the chart and use **Edit | Copy**. Close Excel, return to the Word document and use **Edit | Paste** to insert the chart.*

Exercise 50 - Formatting Objects

Guidelines:

Imported objects should always be positioned within the page margins, as you have done in the previous exercises. Sometimes it may be necessary to apply a border or shading to a data file, image or chart.

Actions:

1. Using the document **Integration**, as modified in the last exercise, select the image beneath the title.

2. To apply a border to the image, select **Format | Borders and Shading**.

3. Select the **Shadow Setting**, the single line **Style**, the **Color Orange** and the **Width ½ pt**.

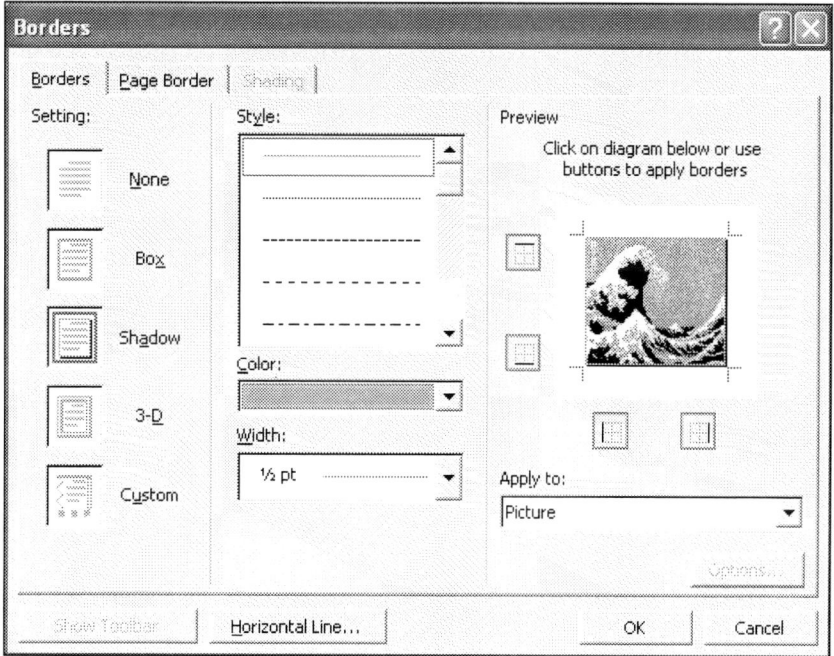

4. Click **OK**.

5. Select the spreadsheet extract.

6. Select **Format | Borders and Shading**.

7. Apply a **Box** border and change the **Color** to **Black** (leave all other settings as default) and click **OK**.

8. The formatting of imported charts can also be modified. Double click within the chart area to prepare it for editing.

continued over

Exercise 50 - Continued

9.   The **Chart** toolbar is displayed and the **chart** appears with a striped border around it to indicate that formats can be edited. Change the display to **200%** using the **Zoom** button drop down list, so that the small text can be seen more clearly.

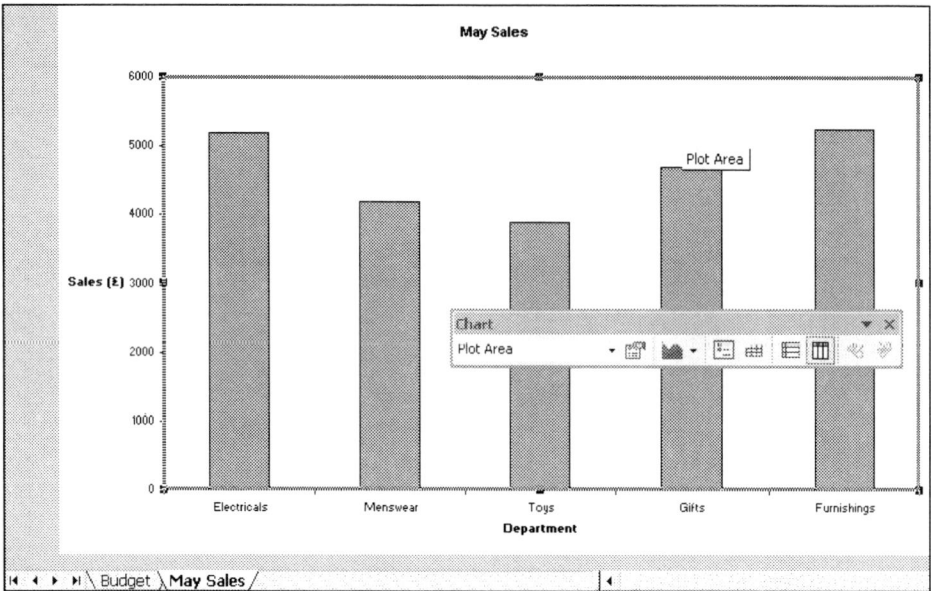

10.   Right click on the vertical axis title, **Sales (£)**.

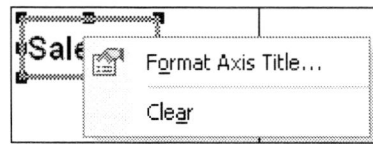

11.   Click **Format Axis Title** on the menu to display a dialog box.

12.   Select the **Font** tab and change the Font to **Times New Roman**, size **12pt**.

13.   Click **OK** to apply the changes.

Note: All aspects of the chart, e.g. axes, titles, background, can be reformatted in a similar manner.

14.   Click on the document away from the chart to remove the border and end editing.

15.   Change the **Zoom** back to **100%** and save the document with the same name.

16.   Leave the document **Integration** open for the next exercise.

Exercise 51 - Printing the Complete Document

Guidelines:

Once the document has all required elements imported and has been previewed it is ready to be printed. Various print options are available.

Actions:

1. Use the **Integration** document, which should still be open from the previous exercise. Click **Print Preview**, to see how the document will look when printed.

2. At the moment, it is not well spaced or finished. Do not worry about this at the moment. Click Close to close **Print Preview**.

3. The easiest way to print is to use the **Print** button, . A single copy of the entire document will be printed, whether it has one page or one hundred pages. Click to print the document.

4. Sometimes, it may be necessary to print only part of a document, or perhaps more than one copy. Make sure page the cursor is in page **1**.

5. Select **File | Print** to display the **Print** dialog box.

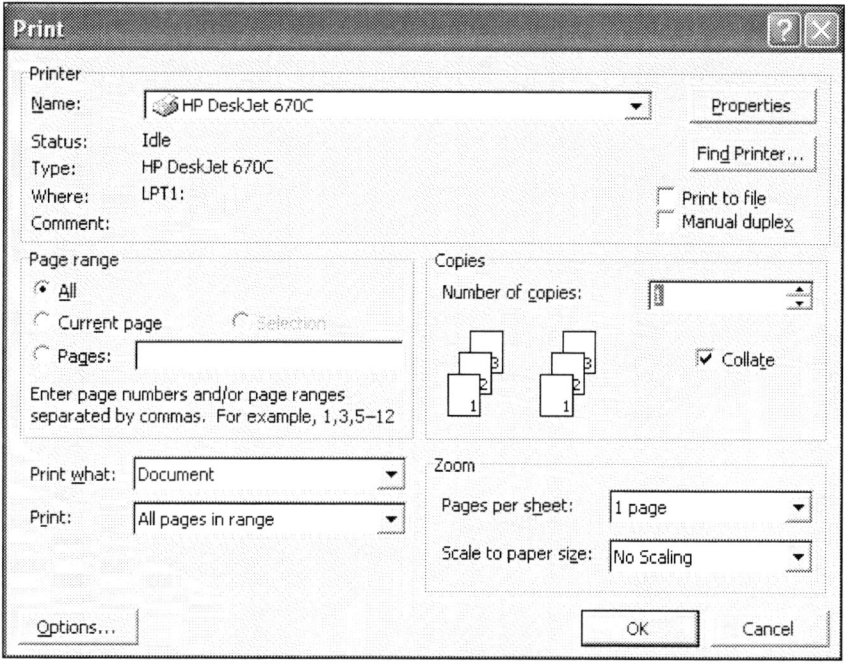

6. Make the options are as above, the defaults. Change the **Number of copies** to **2** and click **OK** to print

7. Save the document and then close it.

Exercise 52 - Revision

1. Open the document **Draft2**. This is a letter between travel agents, about one of their French properties.

2. You are required to insert three objects. Follow the instructions that are displayed in the **Comment** boxes.

3. Insert the spreadsheet **Bookings.xls** where indicated.

4. Make sure it is centred between the margins.

5. Apply a border to the spreadsheet.

6. Insert the picture file **gite.gif** where indicated, resize it to about half its original width and centre it.

7. Insert the chart file **Guest Bookings.xls** where indicated.

8. Centre it and resize it if necessary.

9. Beneath the chart, enter the following text:

   Room 2 has recently been refurbished with a beautiful new en suite and the bookings have increased significantly from last season. Check the previous report on Le Lavandou to see the figures.

10. Print the document.

11. Save it as **Revision47** and close it.

Note: *A sample of the finished document is shown in the Answers at the back of the guide.*

Section 6

Finishing Documents

By the end of this Section you should be able to:

Understand the Function of House Style

Change Page Orientation

Change Margins

Create Page and Paragraph Breaks

Apply Line and Paragraph Spacing

Apply Bullets and Numbering

Insert Symbols

Search and Replace Text

Exercise 53 - House Style

Guidelines:

House Style refers to the guidelines specified for the production of a document. These include paper size and orientation, margins, headers and footers, line and paragraph spacing, text styles (font and size) and instructions on the positioning and formatting of objects.

You will probably come across the term **serif** or **sans serif** when referring to fonts. A serif font is one with curls or tails on the stalks of letters, e.g. **f**, and sans serif is one without, e.g. **f**. **Arial** is an example of a sans serif font and **Times New Roman** is an example of a serif font.

It is essential to follow the specifications to the letter, or marks will be deducted during the assessment.

House Style Sheet - Example

- Use A 4 paper

- Use portrait orientation

- Paper size   12cm wide
  20cm tall

- Margins   top   1cm
  bottom   1cm
  left   1cm
  right   1cm

- Header   flush to left   your name
  centre   today's date using automatic date field
  flush right   centre number

- Footer   centre   page number beginning with 2
  flush right   filename

- Text Styles

FEATURE	FONT	FONT SIZE	STYLE	ALIGNMENT
Main Heading	Sans Serif	24-26	Bold	Centred
Sub Heading	Sans Serif	14-18	Italic	Left
Body	Sans Serif	12		Left
Bullet text	Sans Serif	11	Italic	Left
Table text	Sans Serif	10		Left

Exercise 54 - Page Orientation

Guidelines:

Page orientation simply refers to which way the document is printed. It can be in **Portrait**, , or **Landscape**, mode.

Actions:

1. Open the document **Explanation** and switch to **Print Layout View**.

2. **Print Preview** the document. It is in **Portrait** mode. This is the default orientation.

3. To change to **Landscape**, select **File | Page Setup** and select the **Margins** tab.

4. From **Orientation**, choose the **Landscape** option.

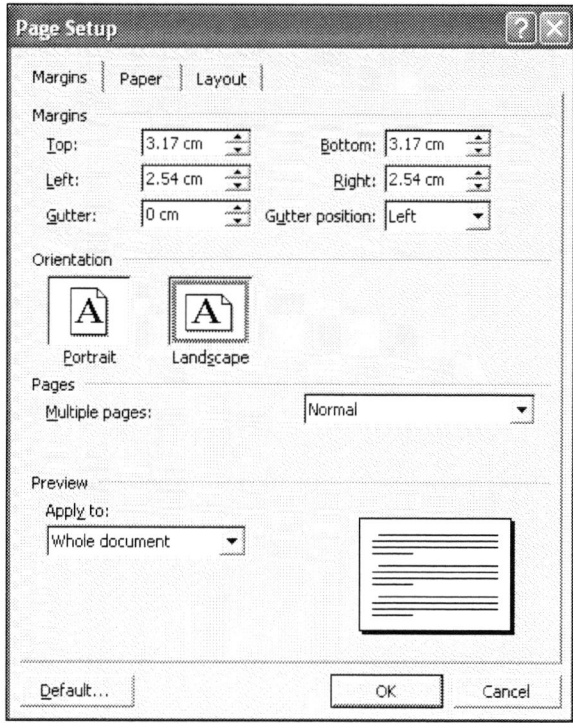

5. Click **OK** to change the orientation. Check the preview.

6. Close **Print Preview** and print the document.

7. Close the document <u>without</u> saving.

Exercise 55 - Margins

Guidelines:

Margins determine the distance between the text and the edges of the paper and are usually the same for the whole document. The top and bottom margins are reserved for features such as headers, footers and page numbering. A large top margin can be set when working with headed notepaper. The top and bottom margins are, by default, set to 2.54cm.

Side margins can be changed to allow space for binding (**Gutter margin**), to change the length of the document and to improve its readability. By default, the side margins (left and right) are set at 3.17cm.

Margins can be altered in **Print Preview** by clicking on the margin boundaries and dragging.

Actions:

1. Open the document **Desiderata**.

2. Select **File | Page Setup** and the **Margins** tab.

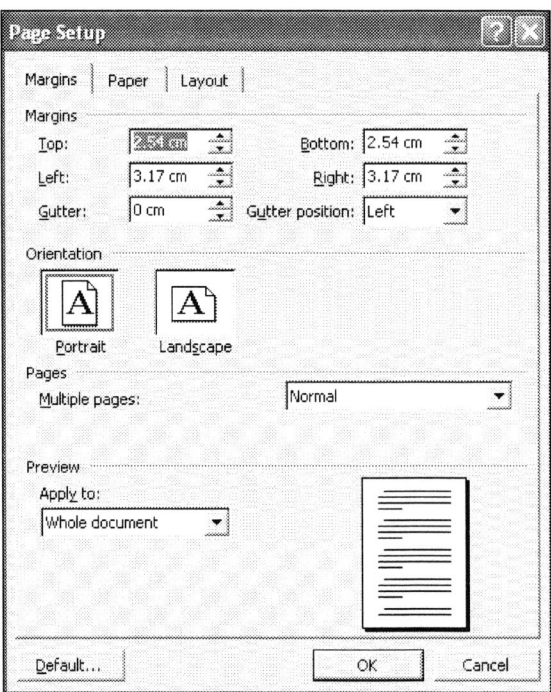

3. Increase the left and right margins to **6cm** either by editing the numbers or by using the up and down arrows. Click **OK**.

Note: *There is an option to use the defined margins for the whole document, or from* **This Point Forward** *in the* **Apply to** *box.*

continued over

Exercise 55 - Continued

4. Preview the document. Notice how it is now goes into a second page.

5. Print the document.

6. Make sure the document is in **Print Preview**. Choose to display one page.

7. Adjust the left margin by positioning the cursor over the margin boundary, on the ruler at the top of the screen, until it becomes a double-headed arrow. Drag the pointer to the left.

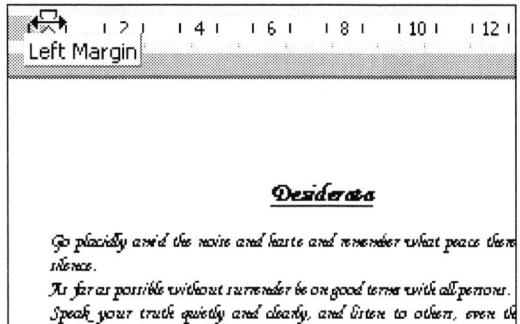

8. Try holding down **<Alt>** while dragging the margin. The measurements are displayed in the ruler.

9. Adjust the top margin using the boundary at the left of the screen. The pointer will change to a double-headed arrow.

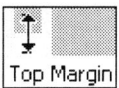

10. Double click on the margin to view the **Page Setup** dialog box, from which the margins can also be changed. Click **Cancel** to remove the dialog box.

11. Close **Print Preview** to see the results of the changes.

12. Close **Desiderata** <u>without</u> saving the changes.

Exercise 56 - Page and Paragraph Breaks

Guidelines:

It may be necessary to start a new page by choice. This is known as forcing a new page. When a **Page Break** is inserted in **Normal** view, a dotted line appears in the text, where the break has been inserted. If this is done in **Print Layout** view, a new page appears on the screen. A paragraph break is sometimes inserted to split an existing paragraph into multiple ones, or to create a new paragraph when typing.

Actions:

1. Open the document **Discovery**.

2. Divide the document into two pages by forcing a new page after the second paragraph. Position the cursor in front of paragraph **3**, then select **Insert | Break**.

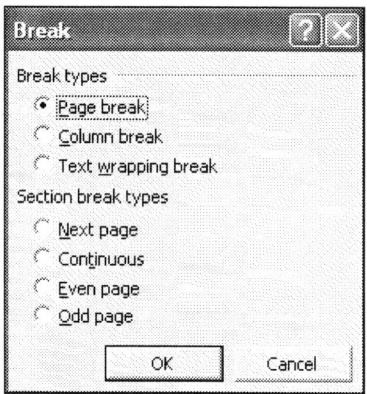

3. Select **Page break** from the dialog box, then click **OK**.

Note: Page breaks can also be inserted by placing the cursor in the correct position and pressing <Ctrl Enter>.

4. **Print Preview** the document to see the two pages.

5. Close **Print Preview**.

6. On page **2**, a new paragraph is to be created. Place the cursor in front of **Tutankhamun's bandaged body**.

7. Press **<Enter>** once to start a new line, then again to create the paragraph.

8. Print the document, then close it <u>without</u> saving.

Exercise 57 - Line and Paragraph Spacing

Guidelines:

The appearance and readability of a document can be improved by changing line spacing. By default, line spacing is **Single**; other commonly used spacing is **Double** and 1½.

Spacing before and after a paragraph can also be changed. Spacing is measured in **points**: **12pt** is equal to one line for a size 12 font. **Widows and Orphans** is a control that prevents *Word* from separating the last line of a paragraph and printing it at the top of a new page (widow), or separating the first line of a new paragraph and leaving it at the bottom of the current page (orphan). By default, the control is on, but you should check the **Line and Page Breaks** tab in the **Paragraph** dialog box to make sure.

Actions:

1. Open the file **Explanation**.

2. Add your name to the end of the document.

3. Select all of the text, then select **Format | Paragraph** to display the **Paragraph** dialog box.

4. Make sure the **Indents and Spacing** tab is selected.

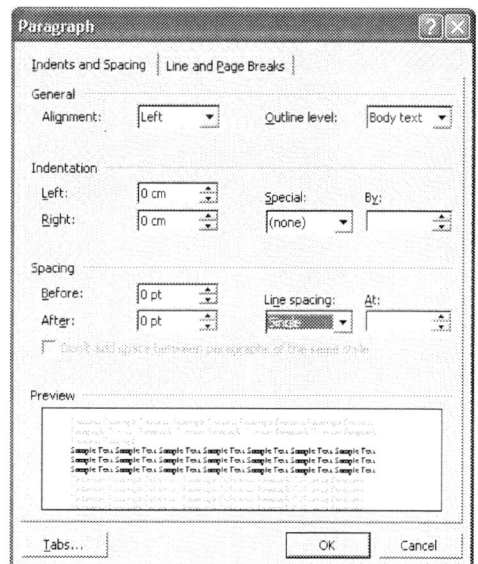

5. Change the **Line Spacing** to **Double**. Notice how the **Preview** at the bottom of the dialog box changes.

Note: The ***At Least, Exactly*** and ***Multiple*** options in the ***Spacing*** area prompt for a value in the ***At*** box. Enter the required value to determine the amount of space between the lines.

continued over

Exercise 57 - Continued

6.   Select the **Line and Page Breaks** tab and make sure **Widow/Orphan control** is checked and then click **OK**.

7.   Justify the text. It is now much easier to read.

8.   **Print Preview** the document and then print a copy.

9.   Save the document as **Explanation2**.

10.   Change the spacing of the first paragraph to **1.5** lines by placing the cursor anywhere within it and pressing **<Ctrl 5>**.

Note: Press <Ctrl 1> for single spacing and <Ctrl 2> for double spacing.

11.   Print out a copy of the amended document.

12.   Close it <u>without</u> saving.

13.   Open the document **Discovery**.

14.   Select the entire document, then select **Format | Paragraph**. Click on the **Indents and Spacing** tab if not displayed.

15.   Paragraph spacing is changed in the **Spacing** area of the **Paragraph** dialog box. To increase the spacing before the paragraphs, increase the **Before** option to **24pt**.

16.   To leave spacing after the paragraphs, increase the **After** option to **12pt**.

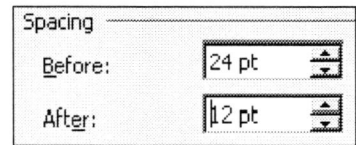

17.   Click **OK**.

Note: To increase the spacing before a paragraph to single line spacing, select the paragraph and press <Ctrl 0> (zero). The same key press will remove this line spacing before a paragraph.

18.   Print the document and then close <u>without</u> saving.

Exercise 58 - Applying Numbers and Bullets

Guidelines:

Lists and paragraphs can automatically be numbered or bulleted. In each case, a hanging indent is also applied. This separates the text from the numbering and improves the appearance of the document.

If an item is removed from the list, the remaining items are automatically renumbered.

Actions:

1. Open the document **Organiser**.

2. Select all of the text.

3. Number it by clicking on the **Numbering** button, ▦.

4. Delete item number **5**, referring to **Mr Parrot**. Notice how the remaining items are renumbered.

5. Print the document and close it <u>without</u> saving.

6. Open the document **Discovery**.

7. Select all of the paragraphs, but not the title and click ▦. The paragraphs are numbered.

8. Now select the paragraphs again and click ▦ again to remove the numbering.

9. Click on the **Bullets** button, ▦, to bullet the paragraphs.

10. Print the document.

11. Close it <u>without</u> saving the changes.

Exercise 59 - Inserting Symbols

Guidelines:

Some situations call for special characters, like é and ô. Some characters and other symbols are not available directly from the keyboard.

Actions:

1.   Start a new document and choose the **Insert | Symbol** command to display the **Symbol** dialog box.

2.   Select the **Symbols** tab, if it is not already selected.

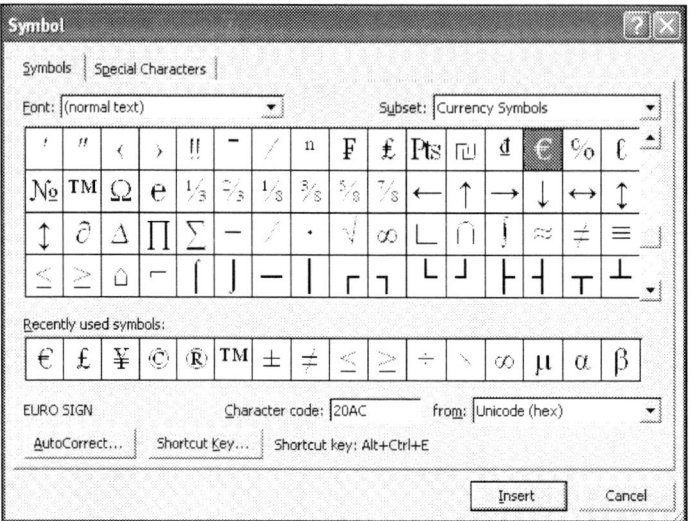

3.   Select one of the symbols. Position the symbol in the document at the insertion point, by either double clicking on it, or click once, then click **Insert**.

4.   Select each of the fonts in turn and look at the range of available symbols - there are hundreds. Insert a few.

5.   Select the **Special Characters** tab. The list of characters also contains a list of shortcut key presses. Insert a **Trademark** ™ symbol. Select **Close** to exit the **Symbol** dialog box.

6.   The size of these symbols can be changed like any other character. Select them and change their size to **16 pt**.

7.   Close the document <u>without</u> saving and open the document **Characters**.

8.   Replace all the character definitions (in bold) with the special characters themselves.

9.   Print the document and save it as **Characters2** before closing it.

Exercise 60 - Search and Replace

Guidelines:

Visually searching for a word or phrase in a document can be tedious. The **Find** command moves directly to a specific word or string of characters. The **Replace** facility gives the option to exchange each occurrence of a particular word, or string of words, with an alternative.

Actions:

1. Open the document **Explanation** and make sure the cursor is at the beginning of the document.

2. Select **Edit | Find**. The **Find and Replace** dialog box is then displayed.

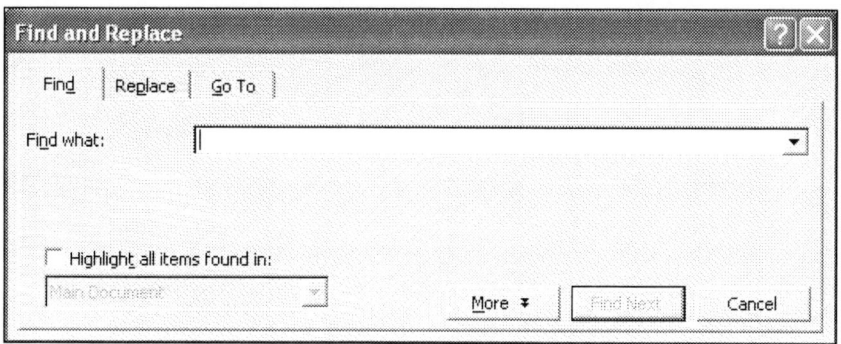

3. Use the **Find** tab and in the **Find what** box, enter **information** and click **Find Next**. The first occurrence of the word is highlighted.

A database is a vast store of **information**.

4. Click **Find Next** again to move to the next occurrence.

5. In this way, find all occurrences of the word **information**.

6. When the **Word has finished searching the document** prompt appears, select **OK**.

7. Close the **Find and Replace** dialog box by clicking ⊠.

Note: To view the **Find and Replace** dialog box more quickly, press **<Ctrl F>**, or click on the **Select Browse Object** button, ⊟ (scroll bar at bottom right) and then click on 🔍.

8. Now, with the cursor at the beginning of the text, find all occurrences of the word **text**.

continued over

Exercise 60 - Continued

9.   Click **OK** at the prompt when the search is complete and close the dialog box.

10.   To replace the word **graphics** with **pictures**, select **Edit | Replace** (don't forget to use ⬇ to extend the menus). Enter **graphics** in the **Find what** box and **pictures** in **Replace with** box.

Note: *<Ctrl H> will also reveal the **Find and Replace** dialog box.*

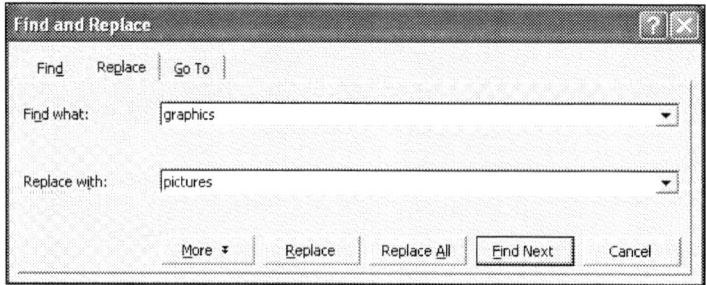

11.   Select **Find Next** and click **Replace**.

Note: ***Replace All** will quickly replace all occurrences of the specified text.*

12.   Continue through the document, replacing all occurrences of **graphics**. When the replacement is complete, one of the following dialog boxes will appear, depending on whether **Replace** or **Replace All** is selected:

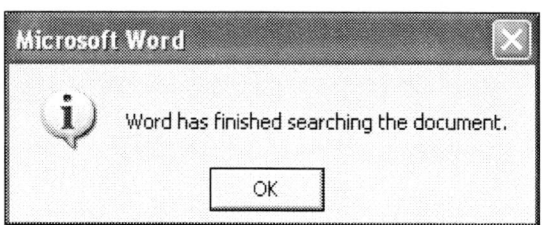

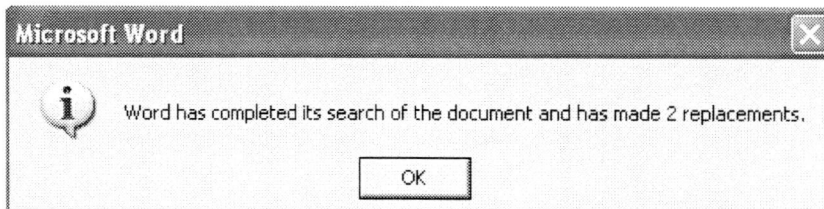

13.   Click **OK** from either box then click **Close** to close the **Find and Replace** dialog box.

14.   Save the document as **Replaced** and close it.

Note: *This feature can save time when typing a particular word or phrase repeatedly. Replace the word/phrase with **#** or a similar key press and, when the document is complete, use **Find and Replace** to change all occurrences of **#**. E.g., **DVLA** could be replaced by **Driving Vehicle Licensing Authority** in this way.*

Exercise 61 - Revision

1.   Open the document **Integration**. This document was created in **Section 4**, but has been supplied on disk as **Revision56** if you did not complete this section.

2.   Apply the following house style to the document:

    Portrait orientation

    Margins – top, bottom, left and right **2cm**

    Header – automatic page number, centred, but not on first page

    Footer – your name, file name, automatic date field (dd-mm-yy)

    Use single line spacing

    Spacing after all paragraphs **12pt**

    Spacing after inserted objects **12pt**

    All objects between page margins

    Text Style (fonts) – centred.   Heading: Times New Roman 14pt, bold and

           Body text: Times New Roman 11pt, justified

3.   Save the document as **Integration Complete**.

4.   Print the document and close it.

Answers

Exercise 10

Step 4   **.doc**, **.xls**, **.mdb**, **.txt**, **.gif** and **.csv**.

Exercise 24

Step 4 - Alphabetically, the last item will be **You are a child of the universe...**

Exercise 45

Step 1   A main document and a data source.

Step 6   5 letters are produced.

Exercise 52

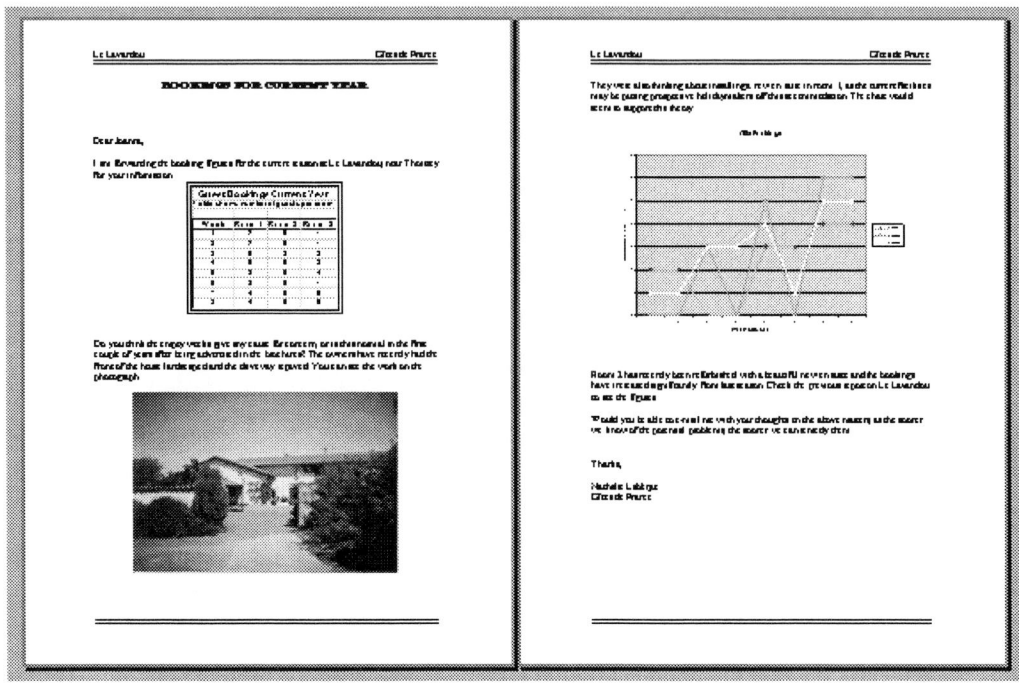

Glossary

Base Document	File into which other objects will be imported to produce the final document.
Browse	Look through all possible storage locations to find the required file or object.
Chart	Pictorial representation of numerical data.
Decimal Tab	A tab used to align a column of figures by their decimal point.
Deselect	Click the mouse button with the cursor away from a selected item so that it is no longer selected.
File Extension	3 characters following every file name, which define what type of file it is and also what application will be used by default to open it.
Folder View	View of computer contents showing a structured list of folders at the left.
Icon	Small picture representing an object such as a file, folder, or program.
Justification	A method of formatting a block of text so that both left and right edges are aligned.
Multiple Selection	Selecting several files and/or folders from a display so that an action can be applied to all of them.
My Computer	A folder available in all versions of *Windows*, which is the default location for storing user data.
Print Preview	Allows a user to see on screen how a document will look when printed.
Print Queue	A list of print requests waiting to be processed by a printer.
Recycle Bin	An area of storage where deleted files are held temporarily before being deleted completely.
Shortcut	An icon (usually found on the **Desktop** area) which opens an application, file or folder stored elsewhere.
Subfolder	A folder that is contained within another folder.
Symbol	A character which can be used in text but is not normally found on the keyboard.
Tab	A way of lining up items in a list of text.
Taskbar	By default, a bar running the length of the **Desktop**, at the bottom of the screen. Shows which tasks the computer is performing.
Word Processor	An application for the creation and manipulation of text documents.

Index

Record of Achievement Matrix

This Matrix is to be used to measure your progress while working through the guide. This is a self assessment process, you judge when you are competent. Remember that afterwards there is an assessment to test your competence.

Tick boxes are provided for each feature. 1 is for no knowledge, 2 is for some knowledge and 3 is for competent. A section is only complete when column 3 is completed for all parts of the section.

Tick the Relevant Boxes **1**: No Knowledge **2**: Some Knowledge **3**: Competent

Section	No	Exercise	1	2	3
1 Manage Files & Folders	1	Folders and Disks			
	2	Folder View			
	3	Deleting Files			
	4	The Recycle Bin			
	5	Archiving Files			
	6	Opening and Closing Files			
	7	Saving Files			
	8	Producing Evidence			
	9	Printing Documents			
2 Enter and Amend Data	11	Entering Text and Numbers			
	12	Inserting and Deleting Text			
	13	Cut, Copy and Paste			
	14	Moving and Copying Text			
	15	Automatic Spell Checking			
	16	Spell Checker			
	17	Grammar Checker			
	18	Headers and Footers			
	19	Fields			
	20	Using Fields			
	21	Working with Fields			
	22	Updating Fields			
	23	Protecting Files			
3 Work with Tabular Data	25	Tabs			
	26	Tab Alignment			
	27	Tables			
	28	Entering Text			
	29	Move or Resize a Table			
	30	Selecting Cells			
	31	Deleting a Table			
	32	Changing Column Width/Row Height			

Other Products from CiA Training

If you have enjoyed using this guide you can obtain other products from our range of over 100 titles. CiA Training Ltd is a leader in developing self-teach training materials and courseware.

Open Learning Guides

Teach yourself by working through them in your own time. Our range includes products for: Windows, Word, Excel, Access, Works, PowerPoint, Project, Lotus 123, Lotus Word Pro, Internet, FrontPage and many more... We also have a large back catalogue of products, including PageMaker, Quattro Pro, Paradox, Ami Pro, etc. please call for details.

ECDL & ECDL Advanced

We produce accredited training materials for the European Computer Driving Licence (ECDL) qualification, for both the Standard and Advanced syllabus. In 2001 we became one of the first companies in the world to obtain accreditation for the ECDL Advanced modules.

New CLAIT, CLAIT Plus & CLAIT Advanced

Open learning packages are now available for the new OCR New CLAIT, CLAIT Plus & CLAIT Advanced qualifications. These packages enable the user to learn the features needed to pass the assessments using a gradual step by step approach.

e-Citizen

Courseware for this exciting new qualification is available now. Students will become proficient Internet users and participate confidently in all major aspects of the online world with the expert guidance of this handbook. Simulated web sites are also supplied for safe practice before tackling the real thing

Trainer's Packs

Specifically written for use with tutor led I.T. courses. The trainer is supplied with a trainer guide (step by step exercises), course notes (for delegates), consolidation exercises (for use as reinforcement) and course documents (course contents, pre-course questionnaires, evaluation forms, certificate template, etc). All supplied on CD with the rights to edit and copy the documents.

Purchasing Options

The above publications are available in a variety of purchasing options; as single copies, class sets and or site licences. However, Schools Editions and Trainer's Packs are only available as site licences.

More Information

CiA have been successfully providing IT training materials since 1985. New products are constantly being developed; please call to be included on our mailing list. Information about all these materials can be viewed at *www.ciatraining.co.uk*.

Notes